Miss *Rush-Rush*

WHERE LOVE LED HER

RUTH STRANEX DEETH

WESTBOW
PRESS®
A DIVISION OF THOMAS NELSON
& ZONDERVAN

Cover design: Cara Samantha Aranas

THE HOLY BIBLE, NEW INTERNATIONAL VERSION®, NIV® Copyright © 1973, 1978, 1984, 2011 by Biblica, Inc.® Used by permission. All rights reserved worldwide.

This book is a work of non-fiction. Unless otherwise noted, the author and the publisher make no explicit guarantees as to the accuracy of the information contained in this book and in some cases, names of people and places have been altered to protect their privacy.

WestBow Press books may be ordered through booksellers or by contacting:

WestBow Press
A Division of Thomas Nelson & Zondervan
1663 Liberty Drive
Bloomington, IN 47403
www.westbowpress.com
1 (866) 928-1240

ISBN: 978-1-5127-6786-5 (sc)
ISBN: 978-1-5127-6787-2 (hc)
ISBN: 978-1-5127-6785-8 (e)

Library of Congress Control Number: 2016920527

Print information available on the last page.

WestBow Press rev. date: 01/16/2017

Acknowledgements

I would like to take this opportunity to thank all those who helped me to produce this book.

It was our friend and William's best-man, the Revd John Durnford, who kick-started the venture in 2008, challenging me to aim at writing my story by my 70th birthday. I am now 72! My three brothers in South Africa all played a part, encouraging me and reminding me about our childhood - Mark, Philip and Alan Stranex - also my sister, Julia Anderson. I am grateful for the way you have all always been 100% behind me.

Without BCMS (now called Crosslinks) much of the book would not have happened, and I apologise for being such a worry to them sometimes! Thank you, Crosslinks, for your faithfulness in supporting me and many others since the Mission began ninety years ago.

My thanks also to Elizabeth Towers who edited the manuscript and bravely advised some 'surgery', which helped to make the book more readable.

Finally, thank you, William, for making this a joint project and urging me on to the end.

As we say in Swahili, *"Asifiwe Bwana"* - May the Lord be praised!

Ruth Deeth
February, 2012.

Contents

Foreword by Bishop Mathayo Kasagara

I first met Ruth in 1979, when I was a young evangelist, studying at the Bible School five kilometres from Mwanza. She arrived weekly on her pikipiki, as we call a motorbike in Tanzania, a small blue Honda 90. She would come slowly to a stop outside our classroom and offload her cassette player and other equipment. She had brought it to teach us how the cassette ministry material could help us in our ministry at home in our village churches.

Neither of us knew then - although God did - that a year later I would leave my home village and come to live in Mwanza, to work with her. For the next ten years, three of us worked closely together as a team: Ruth, Daryl Milligan (the Australian Technician) and I. The work was both new and hard, but I learned a lot during those ten years. Then, out of the blue, our bishop told me he was going to ordain me. I was taken completely by surprise! Soon after this, in 1990, Ruth left Tanzania to go to work in England.

In 2010, by God's grace, I was chosen to be Bishop of the new Diocese of Lake Rukwa. I wrote and asked Ruth, "Please come to my consecration service!" I was very disappointed when she explained how difficult that would be for her. In the end, our Australian friend, Faith, came to the rescue and accompanied her on the long journey from Dar-es -Salaam. My wife and I were thrilled to have her there and praised the Lord.

Feeling the burden of the work ahead of me, with no support staff, I asked Ruth, "Could you become my E-Secretary for any English language correspondence?" She agreed and now spends many hours working for me from her home in Ripon, thousands of miles away!

I want to say how much Ruth has helped me in my spiritual life - to grow spiritually, to rely on the Lord, and be made ready for the ministry in which I now find myself. Truly, if you see anyone standing firm in Christ, there are always people who prepared him. In my case, Ruth prepared me spiritually in many, varied ways to serve in the Lord's vineyard.

This book she has written is the testimony of her life and of how she also passed through various stages in her ministry. I am sure you will enjoy her book and be blessed.

Praise the Lord!

Bishop Mathayo Kasagara   January 2012
Lake Rukwa Diocese
Western Tanzania

Prologue

Amin – that name once struck terror into the heart of every Ugandan. In 1975 people were disappearing every day and bodies found floating in Lake Victoria.

Early in May, armed guards arrested a small white woman from a Mission Hospital in Karamoja and drove her 350 miles to Kampala's Central Police Station. They took her down two flights of stairs, the air thickening at every step. A shouting warder rearranged the cells; ten men shuffled out of one cell into another and she was locked in the empty one.

The air was stale with the sweat of ten unwashed bodies. The walls were black, scratched with African names, and the floor was littered with bottles, dirty dishes and stale food. Old shoes, newspapers and plastic bags poked out from under a board - for sleeping on, I guessed. In the corner there was a crude sink and a toilet sunk into the floor to add to the stench.

The door of the cell clanked shut and the bolt slid across. A Ugandan policeman peered through the bars at this little woman standing under a bare electric bulb. I could hardly believe that the woman was me, Ruth Strancx.

I sank down on my suitcase shaking, too stunned even to pray. All I could manage was to repeat in a desperate whisper, "Jesus, Jesus." I remembered the Bible story of Paul and Silas being thrown into prison and singing Psalms. "I'll try that," I thought. I took a shaky breath and opened my mouth to sing Psalm 23, 'The Lord's my Shepherd'. No tune came out, just a croak: "The Lord's..." and I burst into tears.

Through my tears, I dimly saw the graffiti on the walls. "Who has scratched all this?" I wondered. I thought about South Africa, the land of my childhood, where so many black people had been imprisoned unjustly. The thought trickled into my brain – "Perhaps someone who is white has to be treated unjustly to balance things out."

Wryly, I could hear my mother joking, "Ruth will never die a natural death! She can't behave like everyone else. If she trips up, she's sure to be at the top of the stairs. If she falls over, trust her to grab onto a shelf of jam jars – and pull it down with her. If she slips off the river bank, she'll time it just as hippos are floating by. Ruth will never die a natural death!" I hoped her words were not prophetic.

Blackpool and South Africa 1939 – 1965

Student Nurse Ruth Stranex, age 18

In The Beginning

My earliest memory is of my mother, Edith, pushing me in a pram
down a tranquil country lane with hedges each side and birds singing.
I could have been no more than two years old. Alan, two years older
than me, was trotting along at Mother's side. Suddenly, out from the
hedge sprang a man in a soldier's uniform. He shouted, "The Germans
are coming!"

I screamed... then I saw it was my father! George Stranex was in
training during the Second World War and our family had come all the
way from Blackpool to Bovey Tracey in Devon to be near him.

The reason I was arrested was indirectly due to being my father's
daughter. My own Christian faith stemmed from his, and it was my
Christian faith which had led me to a country far from my own. So
when I want an excuse for my maverick behaviour, I go back to my
father's childhood.

Father's parents were Ulstermen who migrated to Blackpool where
they reared "eleven kids and twenty two pigs". My grandfather was well
known in the local pubs as an eccentric; when he was hatching chicks in
an incubator and it broke down at the crucial moment, he popped into bed
and kept the eggs warm himself, handing out the newly hatched chicks at
regular intervals to his children, one of whom was little George Stranex.

Life was tough and they were brought up tough. My father bragged to Alan and me, "When I was your age I could eat tacks and drink turpentine."

He left school as soon as he could, worked in a shop for as short a time as possible and bought an old bike, mended it and sold it for a profit. By the time he was courting my mother, he had a motor bike, coal business and truck, and once he drove her up the post office steps on the motorbike.

My father became a Christian at a Young Life Campaign meeting. He took my mother to the meetings which were her first introduction to lively Christianity. She was impressed by the enthusiasm in the singing and eventually became a Christian herself – on her wedding day! From the beginning our family lived in the light of their Christian faith with many do's and don'ts and some of my father's toughness and idiosyncrasies thrown in. My brother Alan was more serious than I was. I remember the time that he drummed into me the sixty-six books of the Bible, so that we could both win the promised shillings for being the first to say them in Sunday school.

The war was over in 1945 and my father returned home with great excitement. Rationing continued but there was a very special day when it was announced in the paper that every child in Blackpool could have a banana. My mother queued up and we were both given our banana – a strange yellow curved object – and I wondered how to eat it. We both peeled them and set about it. I nibbled mine from the curved middle so that the curved bit went up my cheeks.

I looked at Alan.

"Eat it from one end," he prompted.

That was much easier! It tasted strange but good.

In 1947, we left Blackpool, the church and all our relations and immigrated to South Africa by Dakota aeroplane. We settled in Durban because that was where our father's troop ship had berthed during WW2. Up and down the coast the bush was covered with banana trees, and I discovered that the name for people living here was Banana People. We had plenty of bananas now. Sunny days were interspersed with school and the economical camping holidays, all with their own share of excitement – like arriving at Victoria Falls campsite at dead of night, pitching our little tent, and waking up next morning to find we had camped in someone's front garden!

Within a few years, my father owned a textile salvage factory. He was Sunday School Superintendent and a churchwarden at Christ Church, Addington. Our family began to increase: Philip in 1950, Julia in 1953 and lastly Mark in 1955. We often had missionaries to stay; some came from as far away as Thailand. Lady missionaries often had to share my room, and I pestered them to tell me their stories. We would go to their meetings where I drank in their illustrated talks. Soon I began to feel that I too should be a missionary when I grew up. So I told our minister's wife, Mrs Molyneux, who had been a missionary herself in China, and she encouraged me.

"Why not train to be a nurse/midwife first and then you'd be more useful as a missionary?"

So, at the age of nine, I decided that I would do just that - train to be a nurse/midwife and then be a missionary! I expected a missionary's life to be tough, but I never dreamt it would land me in jail.

One Sunday evening when I was about ten years old, Alan called me in from talking to the boy next door.

"We are going to play 'at church'." (He would be the minister and I would be the congregation.)

He began with "Dearly beloved brethren" from the Anglican prayer book and then we had the sermon, preaching from Psalm 23, 'The Lord is my shepherd'. I still remember what he said.

"There is someone in this congregation who is not a Christian. I'm not allowed to mention names in a sermon, but that person should confess he or she is a sinner without delay, and begin to follow the Good Shepherd."

After I had gone to bed, he popped his head round my door.

"Have you said your prayers yet?" he asked hopefully.

I told him I had, and to encourage him I sang choruses for about half an hour.

But I hadn't really done as he had said and that was not the time when I began my own, personal spiritual journey. I really don't know when that was because I had no dramatic experience. It often came home to me what a bad girl I was, but by the time I was eleven, I knew I had a personal faith that Jesus was my Saviour, and I should follow and obey Him. This wasn't just because I had Christian parents but because I believed myself.

In spite of the fact that I was truly a Christian, my mother couldn't believe her eyes when she read my school report.

"This is the type of child who makes one wish one had taken a lighter profession like wrestling or boxing. Her behaviour is atrocious."

That was my class teacher.

The headmaster wrote, "Ruth has an undoubted influence in the class; it is a pity she doesn't use it for good."

I knew my problem: I wanted to be good, but it was much more fun to be disruptive in class and make everyone laugh. I shed many secret tears after ending up in the Headmaster's office, yet again. But when I left school, I did so as a short, bespectacled girl who had done nothing outstanding - not academically nor in sport or music - whose exuberance sometimes broke bounds and who had odd ideas about religion.

I began my nurse's training at Addington Hospital, just across the road from our church. I didn't excel there either. I always managed to be the one doing something forbidden – like running down the ward, just as the most dragon-like sister came in.

At the end of my first year I contracted an unidentified virus which paralysed my legs and left me with weakness and a limp. When I was well enough to go back on the wards, I was clumsy and couldn't keep up the pace. I needed to rest more as my legs ached continually. This was my first real experience of suffering and I believe it helped to make me a more sympathetic nurse.

With my 'rubber-legs' (as they became known) I had begun to wonder if I would ever be fit to be a missionary. However, as my legs strengthened, I became convinced that God was healing me so that I could continue my calling. So in 1962, I went to England to study at St. Michael's House, a women's Bible College in Oxford. After two years and much heart-searching and prayer, God nudged me to apply to a Missionary Society and offer to go anywhere in the world they wanted to send me. It had a very long name, which had initially put me off - Bible Churchmen's Missionary Society (BCMS for short).

I went for the interview at BCMS headquarters in London and was ushered into the Field Secretary's office. On his desk I saw the completed questionnaire from the St. Mike's House Principal. I felt that I had never made a good impression on her, so I was keen to know what she had said about me. My interviewer kept closing his eyes as he thought up another question. So while his eyes were closed, I managed to twist my eyeballs round and I read, "Qualities of Leadership." In her untidy handwriting she had scrawled her reply, "Not outstanding."

In spite of this the Mission, BCMS, accepted me and told me that I was to work at a bush hospital in a remote part of Uganda at a place I'd never heard of before called Amudat. I would be working with Doctor Peter Cox and Sister Lillian Singleton.

So I returned to South Africa and in March 1965, I waved goodbye to my family at Durban's airport and flew to Nairobi, the modern capital of Kenya. No miracle took place in mid-air to change me into the super-spiritual being that missionaries were often made out to be. I was still Ruth Stranex, who was 'not outstanding', who would somehow have to fit into outstandingly difficult situations; little did I know that it would include a prison cell! What I did know was that God, who had called me, was great enough to be trusted.

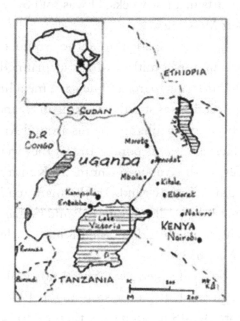

Map of Uganda

Back Door to Amudat

The next lap of my journey was in a Rift Valley Peugeot taxi. These taxis were notorious for packing in passengers to overflowing and driving full speed down the winding road into the Rift Valley to Nakuru with unchecked brakes. The road was a two-way tarred road - no pavements, just a grassy verge where people set up stalls selling their wares like firewood, carved animals, tomatoes, and fluffy sheepskins. At Nakuru I met BCMS mission folk. They presented me with a 'Teach Yourself Swahili' manual and I began to learn. They took me to see the thousands of pink flamingos which flocked to feed at Nakuru's soda lake - apparently the reason for the flamingo's pinkish colour. From a distance the pink edges of the lake seemed to be continually shifting as the flamingos moved about feeding at the lake-edge. It looked like brush strokes of a delicate pink. I picked up a mass of pink feathers which I have kept to this day, still wondering what to do with them.

"You're booked in for the CMS Language School in Nairobi for three months. It starts in a few weeks," I was told by the senior BCMS missionary, Robert McKemey.

But most of all, I was impatient to get to Amudat! The Bishop of Nakuru, Neville Langford-Smith, had a trip planned to Amudat to confirm the first Christians there, and he gave me a lift.

Even though Amudat was strictly speaking in Uganda, the nomadic Pokot tribe who lived in the hills and plains around Amudat wandered freely across the Kenya/Uganda border. In fact they were oblivious that there was a border, so the Anglican Church in Kenya looked after the whole tribe. We didn't enter Uganda by the main road as it was more direct for us to get to Amudat through Uganda's 'back door'; so that is the way we went, through Eldoret then Kitale, early on Wednesday morning, 31st of March, 1965.

With the bishop's wife, Vera, we roared north along a ribbon of tarred road through the Rift Valley, stopping at Eldoret where I was introduced to more BCMS missionaries, then on to Kitale. There the tarred road petered out into murram - unmade, dusty/muddy tracks spasmodically restored by the Roads Department. Again we stopped to meet more BCMS mission folk at Nasokol just before we started the steep descent down the escarpment, from the hills to the plain and over the Ugandan border.

The terrain rose sheer above us on our left, and on our right the cliff dropped straight down into a ravine. We slid round torturous bends, perilously near the edge, and I shut my eyes tight.

The bishop joked, "Open your eyes, Ruth, and look over the edge. That's what happens when the driver doesn't concentrate!"

I saw a wheel-less lorry, bottom up, caught in trees halfway down the gorge. I felt dizzy. In the distance, I could make out a vast plain with toy-sized trees and a faint wavy outline of hills.

"What happens if we meet someone coming the opposite way?" I asked faintly.

"Oh, one of us has to reverse till we find a slightly wider bit," said Bishop Neville airily.

I held my breath, praying that we wouldn't meet anyone. Finally we ground to the bottom – only sixty miles to go and at last I would see Amudat!

The car kicked up a cloud of dust as we drove off along two parallel ruts.

"Here we are at the Ugandan border," announced the bishop as he drove slowly through a 'town' with a few dukas (shops) crouched on either side of the road.

He didn't stop. There was no Customs or Immigration, and we just bumped and bounced our way through the back door into Uganda.

We had to leave our windows wide open because of the heat, but the dust poured in; I felt gritty all over and I stuck to my seat. I concentrated on the scenery: endless leafless, thorny trees with very little undergrowth - I couldn't see any grass. Here and there we passed some odd-shaped termite mounds. Now and again we passed people with firewood on their heads who waved cheerily as we passed, shielding their eyes from the dust we were kicking up.

After about an hour we slowed down as we approached a band of lush green trees. The bishop told me that this was a riverbed where they often had trouble – either it was so dry that vehicles got bogged down in the sand or it was such a torrent of water that vehicles got stuck in the mud. On this occasion we skidded through with no problems, and I couldn't imagine how it could ever be as bad as he said. But I was to get used to this capricious Alakas River, which we sometimes would have to wade through up to our armpits in muddy water.

"Just another ten miles," Vera encouraged me!

We passed some wildlife – a slender small buck called 'dikdik', a pack of hunter dogs with unruly fur in blotchy shades of brown, and some guinea fowl which flapped noisily out of the way.

It was late afternoon when we slowly bumped into Amudat. It looked very small and insignificant - just low 'dukas' (shops) huddled in two rows with a dusty track between them. People and scraggy dogs sprawled in doorways and verandas to keep out of the glare of the sun, and goats meandered across the road. Slowly we negotiated the rocky road and turned left.

"What's that?" I pointed to a circle of galvanised iron, round huts behind some barbed wire.

"That's the Police Post," answered the bishop. "Those tin huts are called 'uniports'; the government use them a lot because they're quick to assemble, but they get very hot."

We bumped along for a further mile and finally drew up, hot and tired, alongside a hospital Land Rover. We had covered about 400 kilometers, and it had taken all day!

Ahead I could see what looked like a uniport but stretched out and rounded at either end, with a porch propped up along the long side. Very near it, at right angles, was another separate room which was to become my bedroom.

The slim lady with thick brown hair who greeted us in a Lancashire accent was Lillian Singleton, my Senior Missionary - born and bred in Blackpool. She gave me a firm handshake and showed me to my bedroom where I offloaded my luggage.

Lillian told us that the hospital doctor, Peter Cox, and his wife Liza (pronounced 'Lizza') had gone to Kampala for the birth of their fourth child but Peter had a puzzling fever which was delaying their return to Amudat. Lillian was keeping the hospital ticking over on her own.

Bishop Neville looked at me.

"I can't see you getting to Language School now, can you?"

I had to agree.

The bishop went to Peter and Liza's empty house to recover from the safari, while Lillian showed me over the house. The stretched-out uniport was divided by a wall into the living area and the smaller section which was Lillian's bedroom. At the back, a short passage led down two steep steps to a smaller circular uniport, divided into three – kitchen, storeroom and bathroom. We walked through the kitchen with a sink and a small gas stove propped on a tea-chest. Through the back door, Lillian pointed out a narrow path at the end of which was the toilet – a long-drop! Just outside the kitchen was a tall stand, built of stones, with a tank perched on top, where my bath water was being heated, and soon I was enjoying a warmish bath in the galvanised iron bathtub. The water was brown, but Lillian told me not to worry - at least tadpoles no longer came out of the tap.

Refreshed, we all gathered for a meal under a hissing pressure lamp. The wide doors and windows were open to let in the cooling air, and the light attracted every imaginable winged creature to join in the fun. Later we sat out on the porch with the pressure lamp and smaller hurricane lamps. No one seemed bothered that moths, beetles and praying mantises were trying to sacrifice themselves on the lamps; or that they tried to creep up our legs! I kept brushing them off me, but no one else was concerned; I was very much the new girl.

We talked and talked till my eyelids drooped. After they had all gone, Lillian escorted me down the winding path to the 'long-drop'. Then I went to my own little room. There was no mosquito gauze on the windows so I closed them all, but I could still see creepy-crawlies creeping and crawling through the gap beneath the door. To escape the insects, I crept into bed under a huge mosquito net. I could just make out the rest of the room by the flickering light of the hurricane lamp – a wardrobe, chest of drawers, table and chair.

I thought contentedly, "What more could I want?"

I wriggled down on the iron bedstead. The kapok mattress felt cosy and I needed only a sheet to cover me. I stretched out one arm under the net and turned down the flame, and very soon the hurricane lamp went out. I listened to crickets chirping and frogs croaking and, yes, I could hear hyenas howling in the distance - they weren't laughing. I learned later that hyenas seldom laugh; Lillian said it was a horrid sound.

"Lillian seems okay," I thought. "I'm glad she's not one of those bossy 'Senior Missionaries' I've heard about."

Then I fell exhausted into a deep, deep sleep.

April Fools' Day

Early next morning, I woke to the roar of an engine. I flung off the mosquito net, leapt out of bed and was just in time to glimpse Lillian reversing the Land Rover and speeding off; but I had hardly put on some clothes when she was back. She was laughing.

"It's April Fool's Day! Someone was sent up on a bicycle to call me for an emergency. I should have remembered; every year the hospital staff tries the same trick, pretending there's an emergency."

She went on to explain that the doctor had once played an April Fool trick like that on the staff; so now, every year without fail, they played the same one back on the doctor. As he wasn't there that year, poor Lillian was the target, but she had remembered when she was halfway there!

After breakfast, I unpacked my new record player and carried it into the living room.

"Lillian, where shall I put this?"

"I'd keep it in your room if I were you," she replied, unenthusiastically.

"But I don't want to sit in my bedroom listening to records on my own. I thought you'd enjoy them as well."

She looked serious.

"The doctor's children might touch it if you leave it here."

I ignored what she said and left it in the sitting room all the same, and Lillian soon started to enjoy listening to records. But I had missed one of the signs showing the strain she must have been under. Five years ago, she had made this house her own home and now she had to share it with me. I wasn't sensitive enough to realise how difficult she must have found this – a quiet reserved person like Lillian, having to adjust to an extrovert like me.

After she had driven off to the hospital it was so quiet - only birds twittering and a brilliant orange and blue gecko watching me from a sunny flat rock nearby. Suddenly I heard a terrific din and followed the noise to the other side of the house. I saw flocks of sheep, goats and calves, bleating and mooing to be watered...

A group of chattering women and girls were pumping the long wooden handle of the borehole, up and down, with a loud crashing sound. The women wore goat skin skirts and, round their necks, brightly coloured beads and tight metal rings. After about an hour the flocks quietened; they all moved off and peace was restored. The gecko hadn't even moved!

When Lillian came home for lunch I learned that this borehole was our own water supply too, and water had to be pumped up to the house by hand every day. She also told me that people called her 'Chepocoggis', meaning 'Cox's daughter'! Because the Pokot couldn't say 'Cox' they said 'Coggis' and Dr. Cox was 'Coggis'. Their word for 'daughter' was 'chepo' - hence 'Chepocoggis' - and we wondered what nickname I would be given!

In the late afternoon, when the sun was less intense, we drove through the 'town' to Amudat Church for the Confirmation Service. It hadn't been built long and was the work of local people – Daudi, the shopkeeper and 'jack of all trades'; some of the hospital staff; those about to be confirmed; and Peter Cox. It had the familiar 'footprint' of a church - the shape of a cross - but there the similarities stopped. Its stone walls were only four foot high, so that people outside could lean over and see what goes on in a church. The corrugated iron roof was held up with (fairly straight) tree trunks. The 'pews' were planks of wood balanced on concrete blocks with an aisle between.

"Where's the hospital?" I asked eagerly.

Lillian pointed vaguely beyond the church.

"You can just see it over that deep gulley," she said. "To get there you go down into the gulley and up the other side, where the patients do their cooking."

I could just see some white buildings, and that's the nearest I got to the hospital that day.

At the church everyone was excited because this was the first visit of the bishop to see the new church, and the first ever Confirmation. More and more people packed the church and squeezed onto the end of full 'pews'. Pokot men wearing shukas (cloths tied in a knot over one shoulder, hiding nothing) leaned over the walls, watching the proceedings and throwing in comments, chewing tobacco and spitting. On the back row two or three Pokot ladies had managed to squash in, wearing traditional goat skin skirts and the tight metal coils which seemed to stretch their necks. Of course each had a naked baby snuggled conveniently near her breast.

These first confirmation candidates were mostly schoolboys who had started school late and so were really young adults. Rev. Timothy Oluoch, of the Luo tribe in Kenya, led the service. He had recently been sent to look after the fledgling church but, like us, he didn't know the local language, so everything had to be translated into Pokot from Swahili. He and his wife, Mary, were as much missionaries as we were.

On our way home we went through the main street again, with its two rows of shops, and we stopped at a small shop which had a loudspeaker swinging from a wire on its veranda. Local tribesmen were sitting on tiny Pokot stools, listening to the radio.

"That's Daudi's shop," Lillian explained. "He's one of the church leaders, the one who tried to speak to you in English."

I thought I remembered him.

A few buildings along we went into a larger, well-built shop owned by Kanti Patel, a British Indian. Across the counter, the attractive, young Mrs. Patel, in a lovely sari, midriff showing, waited to serve us. She handed over the counter our weekly food box together with the Private Post Bag – a strong canvas bag with a huge padlock. This was our precious link with the rest of the world. Every week, at dead of night, a lorry from Kenya dropped these off on its way north to Lake Turkana and picked the postbag up again on its way back.

As we were about to leave, a woman in a long, brightly coloured dress rushed into the shop beaming and shook my hand vigorously. Lillian translated.

"She says you're welcome to Amudat and you must come for tea sometime."

(It was frustrating not knowing what people were saying and I resolved to get down to my 'Teach Yourself Swahili'.)

Lillian continued, "Mariam is one of the Somali women whose husbands keep small shops. You'll soon get to know her as she keeps having babies!"

We drove home following the same route as the bishop had taken the evening before, past the Police Post and up the rocky track to the uniport which I now called "home".

Amudat Sisters

Ruth with Patient

Next morning, after an early breakfast, we set off the mile to the hospital in time for staff prayers at 8 am. Lillian introduced me to seven smiling young men - John Tait, John Lemu, Charles, Simeon, Caleb, Washington and Andrew - all looking very smart in short white coats. We all filed into the office for prayers. I could hear someone sloshing water around in the ward next door. Then came a strong smell of disinfectant as someone swept the dirty water onto a few struggling blades of grass outside.

After prayers these young men, who were known as 'dressers', scattered to their different areas. They were like a cross between an assistant nurse and a doctor! I followed Lillian into the Women's Ward with one of the dressers to translate for us. All I could see were twelve empty beds!

"Wow, it is quiet!" I exclaimed.

"Oh no, all twelve beds are full; the patients are probably outside."

Sure enough there was a temperature chart attached to a clipboard hooked on the end of every bed. Caleb shouted for the patients; a few wandered in and explained that others had gone shopping! Caleb brought us quickly up-to-date on each patient.

"This one's temperature is down," he said, showing us the temperature chart; and then, "That baby is still having diarrhoea, but the vomiting has stopped; it is probably malaria." (My first lesson on malaria: it often caused diarrhoea and vomiting.)

I wandered around to get my bearings and followed a babble of voices to a veranda with benches on three sides and a table facing them. It was the Outpatient Department. At least thirty hopeful patients were sitting squashed together, while others were milling round the table where a harassed dresser was diagnosing and treating. A lady with multitudinous neck rings was pushing her crying baby into his face. He squeezed eye ointment into its inflamed eyes and tried to record it in his book. Then someone else pushed in; the dresser scribbled something on a tiny scrap of paper and the patient went through a door. I followed him in and saw another dresser there, busily dispensing the prescriptions from huge 1000ml bottles – 'Mist Expect' for cough, antacid for stomach pain, laxative for constipation and 'Mist Kaolin' for the opposite. In one corner a tribesman with a decorated mud hairdo was being given an injection in his buttock; in the other corner a baby was screaming after having had its injection, and its mother was trying to mollify it with the breast.

A short distance away from the hubbub, under some sparse trees, I could see gourds hanging from branches of trees and smoke rising from a line of cooking pots, each propped up on three stones. Patients and relatives were cooking maize meal and beans. This was where most patients preferred to spend their days.

Suddenly Lillian called, "Ruth, can you help me deliver this baby?"

She was in a dimly-lit room, calmly getting equipment ready. I felt lost without a sterile trolley, a baby crib and the familiar Labour Ward set up. However, the baby was born with no hassle. Lillian handed the crying baby to the mother and went back to her ward round. I tried to clean up, wondering, "Where shall I get rid of the placenta?" I spied some outside toilets behind the hospital and, wrinkling up my nose, I dropped it down the hole of a deep 'long-drop'.

By now it was almost lunch-hour. We left the hospital to its own devices and went home. We had lunch, prepared by our cook, and Lillian lay down for a siesta; but I still didn't realise the importance of a nap and cockily thought I was too tough to need one; so I began a letter to my parents. It was still burning hot when we went back to work at three o'clock. At five o'clock we all deserted the hospital again although a dresser went back to the wards later to give out evening medicines.

Lillian and I sat out on the veranda for a cup of tea, then bathed away our stickiness, dust and germs. Darkness came suddenly, as it does in the tropics, and everything mercifully cooled down. The lamps were lit and, as on the previous night, every winged insect made a suicidal bee-line for the lights. We had our supper and all the time I kept asking questions - there was so much I wanted to know!

We were just going to bed when a mournful wailing drifted up to us from the direction of the 'town'.

"Oh dear," said Lillian, "it sounds as if there's been a cattle raid."

Sure enough - soon there was a screech of bicycle brakes and we were called to sort out the wounded. I hung on to the hissing pressure lamp while Lillian drove the Land Rover to the hospital.

The hospital looked strange in the starlight. People were milling around outside with soft weeping and moaning. In the dingy theatre (the room where we had delivered a baby that morning), a dresser had already lit the primus stove and instruments were bubbling in the sterilizer. A man was lying on the bare metal 'theatre table', the sort I used to see in the UK in a doctor's examination room. I suppose someone had donated it from a hospital's out-of-date stock.

We listened to the tale. The neighbouring tribe, the Karimojong, had attacked a manyatta (tiny village). Two men had been speared to death and others wounded, and the Karimojong had driven off a huge flock of goats and cattle into the bush. Lillian began to stitch up the spear wounds and we both wished the doctor would come back soon.

Cleft Sticks and Leopards

What a relief it was when two weeks later the doctor did arrive back from Kampala. My first impression of Peter Cox was of a tall, quietly-spoken man wearing knee-length, baggy khaki shorts and long socks. He looked gaunt because of his illness and had an annoying dry cough, but he was eager to get stuck into hospital work again.

His wife, Liza, was a small energetic woman with a newborn baby and three more small children in tow, all with lisps like their mother. She could speak both Pokot and Swahili and was keen to start visiting the women again and plant her vegetables seeds. We were soon chatting like old friends because, like me, she had been a student at St. Mike's. She told me that the Pokot people called her 'Kama-Stephen'.

"All mothers are called after the name of their first-born; so to the Pokot I'm 'Kama-Stephen', and to the Swahili-speaking townsfolk, 'Mama-Stephen'."

Peter now took over charge, to Lillian's relief, and we were kept busy delivering babies and assisting operations. After work, Lillian and I would go to the Cox's house for a cup of tea. It was an interesting house. One half had been the Colonial Rest Camp; it was made of wood, now the worse for the activity of hungry termites. The other half of the house, comprising the bedrooms and bathroom, was a later concrete building, separated by a few feet from the 'Rest Camp'. Lining the Cox's walls were bookcases packed with books so I was never short of something to read.

After tea, when the temperature was cooling down, Lillian loved taking the children for walks through the dry undergrowth to the sandy river-bed and I often joined them. This gave Liza the opportunity to do some visiting. The children would come home happily tired out and Lillian would bathe them, ready for bed, whereupon Liza would rush home and sing out to the waiting, pyjama-clad children, "Loves, you have a treat tonight: blue cuthtard!"

Sometimes it was pink or green, seldom yellow! They were always thrilled with their menu. It was one way to get milk into the children and disguise the strange taste. (Local milk from Pokot cows had its own unique flavour because there was little water to rinse out receptacles and they sometimes had to use the next best thing - cow's urine!)

Not long after their return, Peter suggested, "Ruth, you could go to Swahili Language School for the last six weeks of the course, if you like."

I jumped at it. He found me a lift on a lorry which had stopped for a rest at Kanti's shop in the main street, and so I retraced my journey the two hundred miles to Nairobi. I had been in Amudat only a few weeks, but when I arrived in Nairobi I felt like someone from another planet - the busy modern city felt so strange.

Seven weeks later, with a little more Swahili, I returned to Amudat. Lillian came to collect me from our main town, Kitale. Ten miles short of Amudat we reached the usually dry riverbed, but this time Lillian had to stop because it had become a fast-flowing river. She looked through the windscreen and shook her head.

"We'll never get through that in this small car." Then after a silence, "Oh, look - someone's left a message!"

She was right. I saw a split stick planted in the ground with a piece of paper folded in it. It read, "If you're not home by five, I'll come with some dressers after work – Peter."

Sure enough, about an hour later the hospital Land Rover arrived with Peter and company. They waded through and pushed us to the other side. Water seeped through the door and they were covered in mud, but all was well and we arrived home before dark. It felt like coming home.

Lillian asked me to try to bring order into the noisy Outpatients while she concentrated on the ward patients. The dresser's record book showed that the most common complaints were malaria, eye infections, neglected wounds, diarrhoea and chest infections, and I began to learn how to prescribe for these complaints. I also got acquainted with the spleen, which till then had been a little known organ to me. Peter showed me how to feel for a spleen by palpating the patient's abdomen on the left side, just below the ribs. I could nearly always feel a hugely enlarged spleen, caused by malaria or perhaps brucellosis or Kala-azar, both common diseases. It was difficult to keep records because patients had nowhere at home to keep their hospital records safe from termites or rain. But we still gave them a slip of paper in the hopes that they might bring it back next time.

I remember one particular morning in Outpatients when everything was chaotic. Instead of sitting on the concrete seat which lined three sides of the veranda, people were pressing round the table, hoping to be seen quicker. An old woman was sitting on her haunches on the wrong side of the table, next to the dresser. She wore the usual beads and metal rings around her neck which glistened with goat's fat to help them ride up and down smoothly.

She called up at the harassed dresser, "My son, put some medicine in this eye quickly. Hurry! I've a long way to go home."

Flies circled around her infected eyes. All around mothers were pushing in, with small children (and flies) clinging to their goatskin skirts. I began to make them get into a line.

Seated on his own miniature Pokot stool in front of the table sat a tribesman wearing just his cloth wrapped round him modestly, probably a respected member of his tribe who felt too important to wait his turn. In his hand he proudly held a split stick with his hospital slip slotted into it. That was a first! He wore the usual hairstyle of his tribe - mud mixed with his hair and shaped into a cap, with designs painted on. An ostrich feather waved from a hole on top. Ten strings of red beads hung round his neck, and his sole garment was the shuka - like a sheet - knotted over one shoulder. On his feet were thick giraffe-hide sandals - very rare and probably made by one of his loving wives. His lower lip was pierced and plugged with... an empty injection phial! What a miracle that he had looked after his treatment slip in a split stick. I was so impressed that I had to break my rule and let him see the doctor first!

I surveyed the scene of total disarray and tried to bring order. I whirled into the middle and tried to clear a space around the table. The old woman would not be moved; the town folk, standing round the table wearing clean clothes, were insulted by being asked to sit with the rabble; the tribesman sitting on his stool looked me up and down and answered me obscurely in his own language. I caught an older herd-boy climbing over the low wall to push into the queue to hoots of laughter from the crowd.

In a voice loud enough for them all to hear, I told the dresser, "Don't treat that old woman or that man or any of the people around the table until you've treated the people in the queue."

All this time the hot and harassed dresser was treating patients for cuts, coughs, diarrhoea, malaria and infected eyes. He was on my side but would never have dreamed of behaving in an overbearing manner. I stalked off to shouts of "Hyena!" and I heard them mocking my high pitched voice. I realised I was becoming a typical, bad-tempered, disrespectful mzungu (white person). I knew that in future I would have to make a very strong, deliberate effort to speak respectfully and in a quiet voice. I never won (the patients never learned to wait their turn) but I did learn to stop shouting!

Well, *usually* I did, but there was always room for improvement. One day when the doctor was away and Outpatients was extremely busy, up strutted Loru. He was a large man with a typical beer-drinker's paunch under his white kanzu (Arab style dress). He was twirling a beaded stick. Loru was a chief and always managed to look important; but today he felt even more so and we all knew why. Since early morning we had heard the women's and girls' voices ululating and their ankle bells jangling rhythmically. It was an important day in the lives of his three daughters - they had just been circumcised.

"Sister, please come and see my daughters; they're bleeding badly."

"I'm sorry sir, but I can't leave the hospital; the doctor's away. Look at that crowd in the Outpatients and all those people waiting for me to examine them! Please bring your daughters to the hospital."

"But we always call someone from hospital when our girls are circumcised and they always give them an injection and the bleeding stops, just like that!" He snapped his fingers.

"There is no injection which stops bleeding just like that!" I said.

He didn't believe me and I began to get annoyed, partly because female circumcision is such a senseless operation and partly because I knew there is no miracle injection to instantly stop bleeding.

So unwisely I told him in a rather loud voice, "You should know better than to have your daughters circumcised."

"Are you telling me I'm doing wrong?" he asked, aroused.

"Yes, I am!" I replied.

The outpatients suddenly went quiet, all listening intently.

"If you want me to see your daughters, bring them; bring them here."

Loru stalked off, twirling his stick furiously. The dressers looked away, embarrassed.

I knew immediately that I had been unwise and went to Justus, who worked in the Lab, a mature man and a church leader. I told him what had happened. He didn't waste time.

"If I were you, I'd send a senior dresser to check that the girls are alright. If they really are in a bad way, you had better go to Loru's house yourself."

We did that and I was relieved when the dresser reported back that they were not bleeding much and their pulses were normal. I hoped that was the last I'd hear of it. But as soon as the doctor was back, Loru turned up and stalked into his office. Justus and I were called in, and Loru went through the whole episode, with some embellishments of his own. I felt sorry for the doctor. I knew I had been right in refusing to go to see the girls unnecessarily, but I also knew I had been wrong to be confrontational. The doctor didn't know where to look. Finally he just muttered something vague and asked us both to shake hands.

Justus ended the discussion by saying, "You both did wrong by quarrelling in front of everyone. You are both 'big' people and should have gone into a room to discuss it quietly."

I had a lot to learn. Not only were the climate and language different but also the customs and outlook of the people. Had we any right to expect people from their mud-and-dung homesteads to adapt to our germ-conscious hospitals? And what about queuing? That was foreign to them too. Coming into a hospital was just a strange and unwelcome interlude in their nomadic lives in the vast bush.

We never won the battles against dirt, spitting and bedbugs. If we had not deliberately accepted a lower standard of hygiene, we would all have left with nervous breakdowns! I noticed Lillian taking a more subtle approach. I would suddenly see her in a ward with a bucket of disinfectant, busily scrubbing a smeared wall. Almost at once a dresser would come and say to her, "I'll do that, Sister," and she would thank him and leave him scrubbing!

More discouraging than the lack of hygiene were the patients who left before completing their treatment. I vividly remember a handsome young woman, Cheporogwe, who brought her baby with an abscess of his jaw. The doctor diagnosed TB and she stayed for two weeks while the baby had daily injections. The jaw started to improve but his buttocks became tender from so many injections. One day, long before the treatment was completed, we were dismayed to find she just wasn't there.

Months later Cheporogwe returned with the child, calling him by a different name, hoping that they would not be recognised. The dressers were not deceived.

She admitted, "I had to go and sacrifice. The disease was coming back in his buttocks."

Caring relatives had sowed doubt in her mind. The once chubby child was now unrecognisable; he was thin and lethargic and a huge suppurating ulcer had eaten into his whole lower jaw, exposing bone. He died after a few days and his mother was distraught; her wailing could be heard all over the hospital.

Another woman I'll never forget was Chepoteltel, a young woman who suffered from fits and often fell in the fire. She arrived at the hospital on the back of a donkey, covered with dirty cloths and bits of goat skin. Huge ulcers had eaten into the burns on her arms, legs and chest, and flies hovered over her wounds. The stench was unbearable. We quickly removed her filthy skin skirt and dressed her wounds; then we put her under a mosquito net to keep off the flies. Her mother was sent off to wash herself, remove her own skin clothes and put on the clean dress we provided, so that she could care for her daughter with fewer flies in attendance!

The next day Chepoteltel began to have seizures which were quickly diagnosed as tetanus. Her screams were frightening. We pumped her with all the correct drugs, sedated her and, to our relief, she began to respond. We were thrilled. However her mother, never very co-operative, continually poked dirty fingers under the bandages. Once she even removed the mosquito net, and after we had put it back we found her inside it lying next to her daughter! She mixed her own concoctions and administered them when we were not looking.

The next day was Sunday and the dresser called me after church.

"Sister, I can't find Chepoteltel anywhere."

We searched all round the hospital grounds and found her under a scrawny tree. The damp strip of gut across her chest told us that her people had just sacrificed a goat. Chepoteltel lay on the stony, dusty earth; her eyes wide and staring; a tense, grinning expression on her face, in a state of a permanent fit. Her burns were wrapped around with intestines from the sacrificed goat. Intestinal contents were heaped on her head and were being smeared all over her body. I could have cried.

The dressers told them all off in the Pokot language, wrapped her in a blanket, and brought her back into the hospital. All we could do was to wash her and put her back to bed but she died that night. Of course her mother was grief-stricken.

Even Christians found it hard to trust hospital treatment completely. It was so much part of their way of thinking that some diseases were the result of curses and therefore needed traditional cures. One young Christian, Isaac, was treated for malaria but afterwards had some typical after-effects like aching muscles, dizziness and weakness. He was sure that he must have been cursed and could only be cured by sacrificing a goat. Pastor Timothy prayed with him and tried his best to persuade him that he would soon get better if only he was patient and trusted in the Lord. Nevertheless, Isaac disappeared and came back a few weeks later feeling much better and convinced that it was thanks to the sacrifice!

Every four years missionaries went back to the UK on home-leave and soon it was time for Lillian to go. She would spend her time with her family in Blackpool and visit the many churches which supported her through BCMS. This meant that I would now be on my own, but I was not worried because Peter and Liza Cox's house was just over a small hill. Also, I now had a dog called Pip - named after my brother - to keep me company.

One night, when I was also looking after someone else's dog, both dogs startled me out of sleep with a frenzy of barking. I lay stiff under the mosquito net, my whole body tense and alert, my heart thumping madly, ears straining to catch any sound to explain the barking - is it a burglar?

The dogs settled down, and for a while the only noise was the peaceful sound of grasshoppers chirping and frogs putting in the alto. Then... *crash!* Shattering glass broke the silence and the barking rose to a frenzied pitch.

I broke into a cold sweat. Trembling, I wormed my way from under the mosquito net and crept to the window; but then, having got there, I didn't have the courage to peer round the curtain. There was nothing I could do but creep back to bed again, perspiring with fright.

"I can't stay like this all night," I told myself, but what else could I do? I prayed, "Lord, I can't lie awake like this all night! Please knock me out..."

The dawn chorus of weaver birds roused me from a deep, deep sleep. I had an excited feeling in my stomach - the feeling you get when something special is about to happen - and I wondered drowsily, "What's so special about today?"

I sat bolt upright.

"Why, I've been asleep!" I realised, and the memory of what had happened in the night flooded back to me.

I was overawed when I realised that God had answered my prayer instantly and given me such a deep, deep sleep in which I couldn't feel terrified any more.

I flung off the mosquito net, jumped out of bed and rushed to see what damage the burglars had done. I was puzzled to find only a shattered pane of glass in Lillian's bedroom window but nothing missing. I examined the shattered window more closely... I could see short yellow hairs around the jagged edges. Then I went outside and there, on the whitewashed wall, just below the window, I saw two big muddy paw prints. The truth slowly dawned; the intruder had been a hungry leopard! The dressers all came to look and decided that because it was the rainy season the leopard had probably come down from the colder Kadam Mountain looking for a meal. Now the poor thing must be suffering from a bruised nose!

To tell the truth, I was very relieved to know it was a leopard. The thought of a burglar plotting and prowling around was much more frightening. This was one of the few occasions in Amudat when I felt really afraid and when God took control of my fear. An even bigger fright was still to come, but not yet – not for a few years!

'Coggis' and Cow's Blood

I was glad when Lillian returned from her leave and I was no longer alone. Listening to Lillian and the Coxes, I began to learn more about the Pokot people and the story of Amudat Hospital.

The Pokot lived a semi-nomadic life as their forefathers had done, wandering either side of the Kenya/Uganda border, untouched by politics and governments. Cattle, sheep and goats meant everything to them and enabled them to live simple self-reliant lives.

Animal hides were vital to them and they put them to a thousand and one uses. They slept on hides in their huts. The women and girls fashioned them into 'skirts'. A 'skirt' was really a small modesty apron tied at the back, with a bigger apron covering the back. They cut the hides into narrow strips on which they threaded beads for their necks and ears. They made them into thongs to fasten the lids of gourd 'bottles'; and they plaited the thongs to make handles. Hide slings held babies close to their mothers' breasts, and hide capes sheltered the babies from the relentless sun. Hide panniers, tied on little donkeys, carried their few possessions when they moved on to fresh pastures. Thick hide sandals protected their feet from the wickedly long thorns which lurked everywhere.

Of course, just as vital as hides was food, and that too came entirely from their animals. Their diet consisted almost exclusively of milk and cows' blood! I never met an overweight tribesman or woman. Their faces were small with sharp features; their legs, thin, wiry and strong.

Few were tall - no wonder, on that diet! I was once allowed to witness how they obtained the cows' blood. I saw a young man holding on to a protesting cow's head, with a thong tied around its neck so that the jugular vein stood out. An expert knelt on one knee and carefully aimed a specially shaped, short arrow into the vein. A stream of dark red blood spurted out and was caught in a dish. A lump of mud was stuck over the puncture, and after a slap on the rump, the unhappy cow leapt away.

"Why do they live on blood and milk when they could eat meat?" I wondered.

Once I found some people sitting around their cooking pots, gnawing bones of roast 'something' and I curiously asked, "What meat are you eating?"

The reply was, "A donkey died last night!"

I realised that their animals were too precious to be killed just for food. Cattle were used for bartering or for a bride-price, but normally they were only slaughtered if a sacrifice was needed – if someone was ill, if the rains were late, or if they needed guidance from Tororut, which was the name they used for God.

I had heard the name Tororut often because it came into all our Christian songs and prayers. One of the first Pokot songs I learnt to sing was 'Our God is good, He is good to me':

Karam Tororut;
Karam Tororut;
Karam Tororut;
Tororut omb'ani.

I knew that to be true!

Although they did not know about Jesus Christ, the Pokot were very 'spiritually aware'. They didn't need to be persuaded that there is a God. He was part of their lives. They believed that calamities were caused by Tororut, the Omnipotent One. When a wife is unable to bear children, sacrifice a goat! When a cattle raid is planned, kill a bull and 'read' the intestines to discover the best day for it! When an infectious disease has ravaged the area, prevent it spreading by a sacrifice to Tororut! It was always such a good start to telling them about Jesus, the ultimate sacrifice!

21

After they sacrificed a cow for someone who was ill, they tied a length of its gut across the person's chest. The meat was roasted over a fire, the aroma of meat filling the air. The older adult men gathered around the fire and ate their fill while the younger men and boys waited hopefully at a distance, sniffing the air. Eventually they too were allowed to eat, and then the women and children ate what was left!

The Pokot lived in large extended families. Each family lived with its cattle and flocks in a 'manyatta' or homestead, all surrounded by a thick thorn barricade to keep out wild animals and the marauding Karimojong. A man usually had a number of wives, depending on how wealthy he was, and each had her own hut. There would also be a hut for the young unmarried sons and another for the children. The old folk were never forgotten either. When they had exhausted a watering place and any greenery, they would pile the donkeys high with cooking pots, gourds and hides and move on. I have known school boys go home for the holidays to find their village no longer there!

Until the 1950's the Pokot had no idea what 'government' meant and had never heard of the British Empire. So when a government officer arrived to tell them to start paying Poll Tax, they slung mud all over his Land Rover. The official left in a hurry.

The government asked itself, "What can we do to show the Pokot we are here to help them and that we are not their enemies?" They decided to do something visible, such as building a hospital, and they thought, "BCMS has been working nearby among the Karimojong since the 1930's. Why not ask them to start medical work among these Pokot and the government will finance it?"

BCMS had the very person to send – Dr. Peter Cox, who had just finishing his training at the BCMS College. He was a keen mountaineer and he had been hoping that he would be called to Nepal - but God had other plans! In 1957 Peter travelled out from the UK on the same boat as his fiancée, Liza. He left her behind at Nasokol on the Kenyan border so that she could study Pokot while she taught at the Mission School there. Peter went on to Amudat with climbing rope, boots and ice-pick, despite knowing that there were no mountains to climb!

At that time Amudat was little more than a monthly cattle auction.

Peter pitched a tent and with help from a builder and a book of instructions he built the big uniport which later became my home. He then set to work on the hospital. While the hospital was being built, Peter travelled around talking to Pokot elders under thorn trees – and they began calling him 'Coggis' because they couldn't pronounce an 'x'. They weren't impressed with the government plan to build them a hospital.

With a shrug of the shoulders they told 'Coggis', "Bring your medicine if you want!"

Undeterred he went on with building the hospital. Peter designed it so that each of the two wards should have a gap at the top of the wall to keep the air fresh. When the first patients were shown their beds, they looked at the gap with horror.

"We'll never sleep there," they said scornfully. "The Karimojong will spear us in our sleep!"

So they rested on their beds during the day and slept at night in a nearby gulley. Eventually - although not fortunately - there was a Meningitis epidemic. Unconscious patients were admitted and put on drips which meant they had to stay in their beds at night! So people became used to the idea.

Meanwhile, Liza was still in Nasokol and Peter regularly sent his 'holey' socks in a cocoa tin for her to darn; but a year later that was no longer necessary as she passed her first Pokot exam and they were allowed to get married! They started married life in the house that Peter built.

Liza was a trained teacher and kept her eye on the many schools in the surrounding hills together with a bigger school in Amudat where the boys could board. Some of these children were the sons of those same Pokot elders who had said to Peter, "Bring your medicine if you like."

They had grudgingly come to the conclusion that it was a good idea to have at least one son who could read so they wouldn't get cheated at auctions and shops! Some of their sons were amongst the first confirmation candidates at that service on April Fools' Day, 1965 - my first day in Amudat.

As well as the schools, Liza also started a club for the schoolchildren, on Sunday afternoons, called Explorers. One day, soon after I returned from Language School, she said (with her usual lisp), "Ruthie, I'm handing Explorers over to you."

"But my Swahili isn't good enough yet!" I protested.

"No problem; John will translate for you."

So what else could I say? For the rest of my time in Amudat, I ran the Explorers, and some of the boys, to our joy, grew up to became very committed Christians. What I didn't learn from the Coxes and Lillian, I picked up over the years from these boys. I shall never forget the boys describing to me what a serious drought was like.

"Sister Ruth, you don't know what it's like when there's been no rain for a very long time!" Samwel told me. "The little bit of grass withers away. The trees lose every bit of green. The only colour is in the sisal."

He pointed to some fleshy dull green leaves with lethal points on the ends.

"The herds become so thin and weak; they hardly have enough strength to look for water. The children get thinner and thinner, and the weak ones get diarrhoea and vomiting."

"Why don't they bring them to hospital?"

Patiently, Samwel pointed out that their manyatta was usually too far from Amudat and the little ones worsened so rapidly. I believed that. I knew how quickly diarrhoea and vomiting could kill children.

"The cows hardly give any milk and the mothers try to make it go further by watering it down. Everyone gets thinner and the mothers tighten their hide corsets."

The boys all put on a display of tightening their corsets over their non-existent tummies!

This is one of the stories of drought those boys told me: "During one drought a fire was started on a special hill near our home. Our fathers believe that it's God's home because on top of that hill is a pile of huge boulders with a dark hole between them that drops far down inside the hill.

"They believe that one of God's spirits lives there and if there is ever a fire on that hill, it will never rain again. Our mothers looked at the flames in horror and beat their breasts; we all cried. The elders sat down on their little stools and held a conference. Chewing tobacco, bulging inside one cheek, they gazed up at the sky, looking in vain for a cloud, but they could see only the cloud of smoke. They knew they could do nothing about the fire, which would burn itself out, but they knew they must do something about the drought or we would all die. God was angry because one of his homes had been set alight!

"They pondered all day what to do. Then the chief announced their decision. 'We must sacrifice to God, Tururut, on the hill, and the boy who started the fire must pray for forgiveness. His father has agreed to provide the goat for the sacrifice. A beautiful young girl must carry a gourd of water to the top.' With hand gestures the boys described the shape of such a girl!

"Early next morning we watched the procession go up the hill: first the elders of the village; next the culprit, dragging his black goat; then his father; and lastly the young girl, proudly carrying her gourd of water. Up to the very top they went. There the boy killed the goat with his spear, took dung from its intestines and smeared it on the trees and rocks around the deep hole. He prayed, 'O God who hears, O God who knows, forgive me for setting fire to your hill. God, who sees and hears and knows, please send rain.' The men joined in the prayer with a deeply grunted, 'Owei,' (yes) after each phrase.

"They burnt the remains of the goat, including the bones, and threw them down the deep hole. Only the hot embers remained. Now it was the turn of the young girl to play her part. She lifted the gourd, bent over the fire and slowly poured the water over the ashes. The fire hissed and the steam rose. As if the sky was reminded of clouds when it saw the steam, clouds began to form, and by nightfall... the rain fell!"

"That is a true story, Sister," said one the young boys on that starry night as we sat drinking tea.

He sensed my doubt.

"Perhaps God answered our parents' prayers because that was all they knew?"

I began to realise how much these boys at school were drifting apart from Pokot life. They had different worries such as school fees, uniforms and examinations. They missed out on important tribal events; they told me that sometimes they would arrive back at the village to discover their age-group going through the tribal initiation rites. They would feel left out!

They described to me the mudding ceremony called 'Sapana', which marked the graduation of boys into warriors. It started with killing a bull. The animal was cut up and roasted over an open fire, except for the hip joint which was smashed with a stone. A special mud was smeared over the boys' bodies and in their hair. The head of the bull was displayed at the entrance to the manyatta for all to see, while everyone eagerly waited to sing, dance and share in the roasted meat. Finally the initiates were given their adult names and accepted by the other men as warriors.

As a warrior each one was eager to 'blood his spear' by killing his first enemy. This would be permanently recorded on his body with decorated spots scarred over his shoulder and chest, which he would be proud to display - rather like a medal! I had often treated men in the hospital with this decorated scarring without realising its significance.

All this I learned, and much, much more, just because Liza had delegated the Explorers Bible Club to me!

"Ven is your Vedding?"

I enjoyed leading the Explorer Bible club, although it was held on Sunday afternoons when the sun was very hot. I would walk there through the sparse shade of thorny trees to the school where we would gather in a classroom with a hot, corrugated iron roof. I had no teaching aids but it is amazing what you can do without them. I drew hundreds of humpbacked cattle which John and I cut out and used as attendance stickers; the schoolboys loved earning as many 'cows' as possible.

Sunday morning services were usually led by Pastor Timothy. The church 'bell' - the hub of an old car wheel without the tyre - hung on a nearby tree. It was hit hard at intervals with a piece of metal to remind everyone within earshot that it was Sunday and time for church.

I remember one Sunday morning that I was not at the service because

I was busy delivering a baby. The placenta (afterbirth) would not come out, and this was serious and could cause bleeding, so I went over to the church to call the doctor. I was hoping not to disturb the worship, but I forgot that my arms were caked with blood! I inconspicuously sidled into church with dried blood up to my elbows, and everybody gasped in horror. I was not popular with Pastor Timothy.

In spite of incidents like this, Timothy and Mary were very kind to me and became my 'African parents'. Some years ago (before they had married), they had both been dramatically converted through East Africa Revival meetings in Kenya. The revival had begun in Ruanda-Burundi in the 1930's. It had spread into Tanzania and then slowly into Kenya. Kenyan Christians, revived and strengthened through this spiritual awakening, were a huge influence during the unsettled Mau-Mau times, and they helped many Christians to stand firm, refusing to be forced to take the Mau-Mau oath. Some had even been killed for putting their Christian faith before anything else.

Timothy and Mary were straight-talking with a strong sense of what was right for a Christian to be involved in, following the teaching of all those involved in the East African Revival. They were outspoken about their Christian faith, with no 'Western' reticence about mentioning God.

Mary sometimes took me visiting with her and one day, walking through the burning sun, she checked up on my soul.

"What has Jesus done for you today?"

A bit taken aback, I replied vaguely, "Well, he has helped me to walk with Him."

I was relieved to see that this answer satisfied her.

Timothy was much taller than Mary - slim with buck teeth. God called him to be a pastor while he was a farm manager in Kenya, so he brought all his practical skills with him and was a great asset. He could turn his hand to building houses and churches, mending cars, playing a guitar and even sewing!

Both Timothy and Mary brought a child to their marriage: Wycliffe and Musa. So with their own little boy, Isaac, they had three boys. Mary was slight and energetic with black hair clipped close to her head; plaiting was considered to be worldly. In a game of netball, years ago, her front teeth had been knocked and loosened. She had quickly pushed them back into place, but they had jutted out ever since. She wore her skirts modestly long.

Mary tirelessly made tea for a continuous stream of visitors, many of them people who needed spiritual advice. After work I often sat in their house, incidentally picking up Swahili and learning more about the local people. I took on the role of Mary's 'girl' (msichana), helping her with the visitors and serving her homemade maandazi (like doughnuts).

Timothy and Mary were not afraid to confront me when something was wrong in the hospital. One day, over cups of tea in their home, Mary said out of the blue, "Sister Ruth, you shouldn't leave the dispensary door unlocked."

"Oh, why not?" I asked, innocently.

"Why does Steven come off duty drunk?" Timothy joined in.

"What's that got to do with the dispensary?"

"What do you use for sterilizing your emergency syringes?"

"We keep them in a dish of surgical spirit," I replied, puzzled.

Suddenly it dawned on me... so *that* was why the spirit 'evaporated' so quickly! Stephen was having a quick swig now and again.

"And why don't you count your penicillin bottles?" Timothy pressed me.

"I don't have time!"

I was feeling annoyed by now.

"Well, you should keep the door locked then. You are not helping our people if you tempt them to take things."

"But why should anyone want to take away penicillin?"

Mary looked embarrassed and hinted about illicit penicillin injections which a member of staff was giving in exchange for money.

Even though I was sometimes put on the mat like this, it was good to feel so welcomed; and I also started visiting some of the families of teachers and dressers - like Mariamu, the Somali woman who had welcomed me on my first day. I would call on them after work, instead of going straight home, and then walk back along the bush paths when the sun felt cooler. These friendships helped me stand in the shoes of people who were so different from me and came from very different backgrounds.

Everything has its drawbacks though! I became good friends with a lovely Christian man who was a school teacher. We would walk to the school together talking non-stop and sit in his one-roomed house, always with the door wide open, just near the classroom where Explorers met on Sundays. We drank endless cups of sweet tea made by his two young brothers. But it was not wise. Rumours spread that we were going to get married!

I rushed into Mary's house feeling very embarrassed.

"Do you know what people are saying about me?"

"Yes, of course," Mary laughed. "We must be harmless like doves but wise like serpents, Ruth!"

I was relieved when the next year he married the chief's daughter, Margaret, a girl from the top class in his school.

When Margaret's mother had been young there was no school. So Mary spent a lot of time teaching her and other women to read and sew. Once she organised a women's course and more than twenty women came to it. Two Ugandan women, both called Elizabeth, travelled all the way from Kampala to teach the Bible, as well as cooking and child care. One of these Elizabeths loved red – as she told us one day, flourishing a purple handkerchief taken from the sleeve of her orange cardigan and wiping the perspiration from a brow crossed with a red nylon headscarf. Over her large perspiring form she wore a pink floral dress which reached down to her ankles.

As usual Mary was scurrying everywhere, organising meals, and cooking over an open fire in her smoke-filled mud kitchen. We missionaries helped where we could. Lillian held the fort in the hospital, while I ran errands, carried pots of tea and served food as Mary's msichana. Liza kept everyone supplied with cake.

The programme consisted of nothing but meeting after meeting and preaching after preaching; so Liza and I tried to liven it up.

"What about a game of netball?" energetic Liza suggested.

Elizabeth (the one who loved red) was horrified.

"God does not want us to fall down and hurt ourselves!"

I had a good laugh at this and felt put out when she turned to me and said, "Sister Ruth, you must repent of laughing so much."

When she went out, I turned to Timothy, giggling.

"What does she mean, Timothy? She doesn't like netball. I can't laugh when I want to. All she likes are red clothes and long sermons."

"Okay, Ruth, calm down! We understand you. We know you laugh and joke a lot and we know you love the Lord Jesus. But just you be quiet! Don't argue; submit as a msichana ought to do."

I was getting a taste of what it is like to be an African girl among her elders! As the years passed I felt that I never stopped being treated like a msichana. I imagined my role might always be that of pouring tea and serving maandazi. One day, when we were out visiting, Mary made me wait outside the house.

"Msichana wangu - my girl - just wait here on this rock; I want to talk to those women about things we cannot discuss in front of unmarried girls."

I was a trained midwife, but my mind boggled as I sat waiting obediently on the rock outside.

At night, alone with my thoughts, I would sometimes panic at the thought that in my present situation I might never marry. I seldom met eligible young men. The Cox family had many visitors, even eligible young men, but they stayed only a day or two and then left before they could discover what a scintillating personality was hiding beneath a rather ordinary exterior!

A friendly Asian shopkeeper didn't help by saying almost every time he saw me, "Vell Sister, ven are you going to make your vedding?"

"Oh, I'm not getting married. There are not enough men to go around," I would joke.

"You lie; your vader has a husband vaiting for you at home. Ven you bringing him?"

Old Gappy (he had parted company with his front teeth at our hospital) said this again and again, and it began to hurt. I had to learn to accept that I might never 'make my vedding'.

Was I going to be Mary's msichana for ever and be forever pouring out tea?

The disappointment of remaining single was never finally buried and popped up in many unsuspecting moments.

A Good Beggar

Single, yes, but not lonely! Life was never dull with the Coxes nearby and a continuous stream of visitors. We had many lively discussions in their home and there were always books to read and music to listen to.

Peter managed to persuade the Health Department that we desperately needed a bigger and better Operating Theatre. It was wonderful the day we started to use it - with its big windows letting in lots of lovely, much-needed light. These windows had a disadvantage though. After a cattle raid, anxious relatives leaned through the windows shouting encouragement to the doctor as he patched up spear wounds!

However, after about three years, Peter's recurrent fevers became more frequent and his cough more troublesome, so he went to Kampala to see his specialist friends. Just when we were expecting him back, the bishop's Holden car drew up and out stepped Bishop Neville looking solemn. He gave Liza the news.

"I've had a phone call from Kampala. Peter must go to England for more tests. I'll take you and the children to Kampala to see him before he leaves."

Liza was unique – no panic, no tears. She cooked a meal for the four children, put them to bed, and then prepared for the next day's safari. At midnight, after everyone had gone to bed, the bishop saw a hurricane lamp bobbing up and down in the garden. He went to investigate. It was Liza.

"I'm just planting out beans in case it rains while I'm away," she explained.

Early next morning, Peter's 'bag' was at the door ready. Bishop Neville stared at it. Hanging from the heavy frame haversack were an ice-pick, climbing rope and Peter's climbing boots.

"What's all this? Peter's ill, not going on a climbing holiday!"

"Oh, Peter never travels without them. He'd be so upset if he left them behind," lisped Liza.

The bishop put them in the car and off they all went.

About a week later we were all surprised to see the whole Cox family, including Peter, arrive back to Amudat plus all the climbing equipment. Peter and his consultant friends thought it was worth trying one more thing - to move to somewhere else with a less harsh climate and see if Peter improved. Everyone was shocked to hear that Coggis was leaving.

Unknown to any of us except God, a new doctor was already on his way to Amudat. Even he himself didn't know it yet! Dr. David Webster had only recently stepped off the plane in Nairobi, destined for Marsabit Hospital in Kenya where David had grown up. His parents had been lifelong missionaries there. He had been looking forward to taking his wife Rosemary to his childhood haunts and introducing her to his old playmates. At the precise time when Peter's future was in the balance, David and Rosemary were at Language School in Nairobi, preparing for Marsabit. It dawned on the BCMS Council that the Websters could be God's solution for Amudat! Letters flew back and forth between continents and the result was that Peter and David agreed to swap hospitals.

Peter and family would go to Marsabit, a cooler mountainous area. David and Rosemary, with little Andrew and baby number two on the way, would come to Amudat - a very hot semi-desert. This was a huge challenge for them both. For Rosemary it was a culture shock as well because she was completely new to Africa, and only her trust in the Lord kept her going.

When they arrived in Amudat, David, Rosemary and Andrew had to squash themselves into the tiny guest house until the Cox's left. During the next two months, baby Paul was born and David began to take over the hospital from Peter. Then we waved goodbye to the Cox family at the airstrip, and the Websters moved into the main house which the white ants had ensured was in a poor condition! Everything settled down again, but challenges, chops and changes were ahead for all of us.

Southern Sudanese refugees began to trickle into a Refugee Camp only thirty miles away, and we were their nearest hospital. The trickle swelled to a flood until the hospital was overflowing with pathetically malnourished children and adults with huge tropical ulcers. They owned nothing, not even a piece of cloth or a discarded tin. At night they lay all over the floors leaving me nowhere to put my feet when I tried to care for them. We needed more wards!

We also needed David's sense of humour. One day, Justus the lab technician came to me laughing and shaking his head.

"I think Dr. Webster is very funny. He has just told me that coming to Amudat has made him a good beggar!"

Justus laughed and laughed. But it was so true. David spent hours and hours writing detailed applications for grants to enlarge the hospital - with graphs, statistics and photos of skeletal children. Then came the rejections and he would spend more hours reapplying, with more graphs and photos. We were desperate!

Eventually his begging was rewarded. Oxfam gave us money for a TB ward, maternity unit, new Outpatients, new laboratory and X-ray building. 'Bread for the World' donated the X-ray machine. The new wards went up rapidly. The walls were put together like a Meccano set. Metal strips with holes drilled along their length were screwed together to make a frame; wire mesh was fixed into the frame and then cement was slapped into the mesh. This was a wall! After plastering the walls, concreting the floors and roofing with corrugated iron, the new wards were ready.

By now the hospital had doubled in size and we needed more staff. One night I dreamt that we took on a certain ex-Amudat schoolboy and jokingly I told the dressers, "I dreamt last night that we gave a job to Silas." Unknown to me they wrote to him.

He arrived smiling. "I've come, Sister Ruth."

David Webster agreed to give him a job.

After a few weeks working with the other dressers, Silas seemed to get the hang of it, although he was a little slow. Then he suddenly went berserk! I was in one of the new wards when I heard a lot of shouting, and I rushed to find out what the commotion was about. Silas had ridden a bicycle at top speed between the beds of two wards, shouting at the top of his voice. Before the dressers could pin him to the ground he had hit out at our short-term Sister, Di Wildish, and had knocked her to the floor.

I was relieved to find Di dazed and gasping, "What did I do wrong?"

Then we found out that Silas had been treating himself with medicines which he knew nothing about. After he recovered, he left us, and I resolved never again to tell the dressers my dreams.

Wives for the Schoolboys

I never even dreamt about the new dimension to my life which God had in store for me. No one sat down and planned it, saying, "Ruth, from now on you are going to help Pokot girls to go to school." God arranged it all!

When I first came to Amudat, there was already a school where some Pokot boys went, and among them was a small, lively group of Christian teenagers. They had heard about Christ at school, and they had enjoyed the fun and teaching at the Explorers Club. We saw them grow spiritually till they made open commitments to Christ as their Saviour. They were very sincere about their Christian faith, and Timothy and Mary taught them to be strong and to stand firm in the face of mockery from other lads.

I came to know many of them well, and they would discuss with me the Christian way of life and the problems it brought. One problem which kept cropping up was about marriage.

"The pastor tells us we must marry Christian girls who have been to school, but where are they?" they asked. "We don't want to be given mugs of tea with flies floating around in it!" joked one.

Another added, "We want them to wash our babies' faces so they don't get eye infections."

They had a solution! Pokot girls should somehow be enabled to go to school, and that meant that a place was needed where they could live in term time. It wasn't possible for Pokot children to go to school daily because they and their nomadic families wandered around with cattle from place to place. The boys at school slept in big dormitories, and anyway the parents would never allow their daughters to sleep so unprotected. The boys suggested that I start a hostel for the girls, but when we thought more about it we decided it was impractical.

But God thought differently! It so happened, a few years later, that a girl of about twelve ran away from her village after her parents died, and she came to live with a relative in Amudat. He asked if she and three friends could sleep in the empty mud hut near my house. Only after agreeing to this did it dawn on me that this was the beginnings of the girls' hostel!

More girls were brought by fathers and brothers to go to school and sleep in the mud house. Quickly the school recognised the mud hut as official accommodation for girl boarders and even provided food. But the more girls who came, the harder it was for me to look after them. Of course, I was working full-time in the hospital and could be called out at any time to women in labour or warriors with spear wounds.

One night all the girls ran away; some of them had eaten all the food and the others were hungry! Another time, one of the girls tried to strangle her 'friend'. I was ready to admit failure. I turned to Timothy and Mary and they saw that my 'remote control' method of looking after girls was not working.

"You need help!" they said.

A 'Mama' was found, called Mary. She was the wife of Samson, one of the dressers, and the family moved to live next door to the hostel. Eventually there were more than thirty girls there, but even with a 'Mama' to look after them they took up a great deal of my time. One dark night Lillian was walking between her house and the doctor's, when she called to me through the trees.

"Ruth, are these girls meant to be walking in the bush so late at night?"

I dashed over and found some of our precious girls round-eyed, squeaking in excitement, "Sister, come quickly. Anna says she's going to hang herself!"

In bed at night, as I was trying to sleep, I often heard rhythmic clapping from the surrounding villages, accompanied by shrill women's and girls' voices and gruff male voices responding in song. A dance was in progress - some celebration - possibly the start of a girls' circumcision ceremony. I knew that the girls in the hostel could also hear.

Did they long to join in? Deep down, did they miss being active members of their tribe? Or did they snuggle down in bed anticipating or fearing the day when they too would be circumcised?

I hadn't been able to hide from them our disapproval of female circumcision, which has no medical justification whatsoever. Delivering a first baby was always far more difficult and needed a large episiotomy cut because of all the scarring.

Were we wrong to encourage the girls to go to school, and to discourage them from being circumcised? Was I making them outsiders? Could modern schooling and tribal customs mix?

These unanswerable questions would whirl around in my brain, keeping me awake even more than the clapping and high-pitched singing.

Idi Amin Dropped In

In 1970, Lillian and the Webster family were all on UK leave and Dr. John Malcolm had come to Amudat to fill in. All seemed normal! But on 2nd February 1971, as we gathered for the usual hospital prayers, Dr. Malcolm arrived late, looking puzzled.

"I can't make it out," he said. "There was no news on the radio this morning, just military music. Do you think there could have been a coup or something?"

All we knew for certain was that the Ugandan President had been visiting Singapore. Justus, the lab technician, hurried over to his house and turned on the radio. He rushed back!

"There *has* been a coup! Milton Obote's been ousted and has fled to Tanzania. The head of the army's taken over!"

I couldn't catch his name as I'd never heard it before, but we were soon to hear it too much: Idi Amin Dada!

For a while, nothing changed. We began to say to one another, "Perhaps the coup was a good thing after all!" Over the previous few years, we had heard rumours that Obote owned fleets of taxis and buses and was stashing money away in foreign banks, so perhaps the new regime would be less corrupt. Hospital life carried on as usual. We even continued to get visits by air. The Flying Doctors went on bringing in Dr. Joe Taylor to do eye operations, and Missionary Aviation Fellowship continued to fly in visitors. The planes would always buzz over the hospital before landing, and someone would leap into the Land Rover and bump out to the landing strip to meet them.

When a plane buzzed over the hospital a few weeks later, Dr. Malcolm jumped into the Land Rover as usual and went off in a cloud of dust to collect whoever it was. This time he returned with Idi Amin! Amin shook hands with me. He was so tall! We gave him a grand tour of the hospital, and he had his adjutant note down the problems we pointed out; then he was off again. We all felt excited and impressed. He was taking a personal interest in the hospital, and it seemed he was going to help us!

Then we heard over the radio that Amin had announced a new law. In future everyone must wear western clothes - no more goat skins for the women or shukas (cloths) for the men. Anyone disobeying the new law would be shot! Only a few days later, Di called me to see a tearful young woman on the hospital veranda, nursing a chubby baby. She was wearing goat skins and had been seen by a soldier who had shot at her. The bullet had grazed her baby's leg and gone through her side but fortunately missed all her vital organs.

Women began arriving at the hospital in a dirty dress, which we recognised as the very same dress previously worn by other patients. The women of one manyatta must have had only one dress between them and they kept it for whoever was going to the hospital or the shops. They hoped that the soldiers wouldn't penetrate into the bush to check their clothing. The Pokot continued their normal nomadic lives, looking after their flocks and herds, the political situation hardly touching them at all.

Occasionally, soldiers with Kalashnikovs swaggered down the hospital veranda demanding immediate treatment. We kept quiet and treated them as quickly as possible in order to get them out of the way. Even I, who had sometimes gone over the top in 'crowd control', meekly kept my mouth shut.

Whispered rumours began to filter through to us about people in Kampala going missing. We even knew one of them. Godfrey was a Ugandan medical student from Mulago Hospital in Kampala. He had done a three-week placement with us, and we had all been impressed with him. He had left promising to keep in touch with us, but he was never heard of again.

During the night of 3rd August 1972, Idi Amin had a dream. On 4th August, my birthday, he announced on the radio that God had told him in this dream to expel all Asians with British passports within three months. He mustn't have heard God correctly because a short time later, he expelled even Asians with Ugandan passports. Their shops, garages, businesses and cars were given to Ugandans.

"This is an economic war," he announced.

We were relieved that 'our' Asian shopkeepers had all left for Kenya soon after Amin's coup. The next we heard of Kanti was that he had a shop in Morecambe, Lancashire!

More things unnerved us. On 14th November, Uganda Radio summoned all British missionaries to report to Kampala immediately for their documents to be scrutinised. By now David and Rosemary Webster had returned from UK leave - now with three little boys. We all dropped everything and piled into the Land Rover, wondering if we would ever come back to Amudat, and we bumped the 350 dusty miles to Kampala. The streets looked strange with no Asians though I did glimpse one young Asian lady in the distance; we gave each other a sympathetic smile.

Gruff officials checked our visas but couldn't find anything out of order with our papers. David did some quick medical business and asked after Godfrey. People just shook their heads, muttering that many people were just disappearing. When we all arrived back in Amudat, everyone was relieved that we hadn't disappeared too.

All over Uganda, army officers were being dispatched as 'Governors'; one even came to Amudat. Road blocks were set up everywhere, manned by junior soldiers, often the worse for drink and heady with their own power. One barrier was set up on the main road near Pastor Timothy's house where he sometimes saw soldiers beating people up. Once he even witnessed a soldier jumping up and down on a man's abdomen; he just couldn't keep quiet any longer and, ignoring his own safety, he went over and pleaded with them.

Because of the road blocks, Kenyan lorries no longer took the short cut north through Amudat; this meant we stopped getting our food boxes and the Private Post Bag from Kitale. Basic commodities like soap, paraffin and cooking oil became more and more scarce and we became dependant on dwindling supplies from our nearest big town in Uganda - Mbale - the only place to get fuel for the generator and vehicles. I was sometimes the one to do that safari. I packed the back of the Land Rover with empty 44 gallon drums, and at Mbale I filled them with diesel and petrol and returned the 100 mile trip, escorted by the fumes.

Daudi, our shopkeeper/friend, got busier and busier as spare parts for engines got scarcer and scarcer. Daudi was a natural whizz at fixing things, especially cars, and over the years he had accumulated mountains of spares, which looked like junk, in his backyard. He was in great demand, and with extreme patience he worked miracles mending our vehicles. In spite of the political situation, he still found time to go to a Pastors' Training College in Kenya. Although he had little formal schooling, he was ordained and was ready to lead the church after Timothy and Mary were called back to Kenya.

In spite of the political tensions, the hospital continued to grow. David Webster, together with his visiting brother, Dennis, and the dressers, built a new dispensary 27 rocky miles from Amudat in a remote area near the foothills of Kadam Mountain. It immediately became very busy with over five hundred outpatients per week. In the hospital we even delivered a set of triplets! Then, to our astonishment, when David was doing a Caesarean Section, we found a baby wasn't in the uterus at all but cuddled up with the intestines (called an 'extra-uterine pregnancy')! Mother and baby thrived.

With all the tensions and uncertainties, Lillian didn't return to Amudat after her UK leave but moved on to another hospital in peaceful Tanzania. However, medical students continued to come to Amudat from the UK to do their 'electives'. Keith Knox was one of these. He was popular with everyone, especially the Webster boys who loved his fun and games. Besides hospital work, he loved spending time with the girls in the hostel, teaching them lively games and English choruses; and on Sundays he helped Rosemary Webster with her large Sunday School. When he left after three months to finish his medical training, the girls all cried.

Ten Little Schoolboys

It was always a relief to go home after work, to get away from the political turmoil and immerse myself in the normal problems of the girls in the hostel. One day when I arrived home from the hospital, a small thin boy presented himself at my door. His skin grey with dust, he wore only a skimpy, grubby cloth around his loins. The girls were helpfully hovering around. He spoke only Pokot, which I still did not know except for the medical jargon, so the girls told me his name – Lomuria - and translated for him.

"Please will you give me some clothes, so I can go to school?"

Rosemary Webster found a shirt and a pair of shorts which had belonged to little Andrew Webster, and we squeezed Lomuria into them. They looked very skimpy, but he beamed happily and the girls enthusiastically escorted him on his way to the school.

My parting shot was, "There's nothing for nothing, you know. Come back and water my garden!"

I pointed to some geraniums, struggling to bloom in five old paraffin tins. The girls enjoyed translating that! I thought nothing more about it and was surprised when he appeared again. Each evening after school, he watered the flowers to pay for his clothes and then went back to school to sleep.

The girls told me in hushed tones, "He's an orphan. His parents were killed in a cattle raid. He stayed on in the village and helped herd sheep and goats but yesterday he lost one."

They went on to explain that he was afraid to go back to the village as he knew no one would stand up for him, so he ran away. I often wondered who had directed him to my door. I bet it was one of those girls! When school holidays started, he turned up at my door.

"Where do I sleep now?" he asked.

It began to dawn on me that he had come to stay!

Gradually he brought more boys to help him do the watering and with similar requests for clothes. I began to hear what was happening each night in the boys' dormitory at the school; Lomuria was praying with his little gang and teaching them the Pokot Christian songs and Bible stories that he was picking up at Sunday School and Explorers. This motley crew came enthusiastically to church every Sunday morning, wearing odd bits of clothing and occupying the three front rows of the church. Pastor Timothy and Mary had by now been called back to Kenya, and Daudi, leading the services, beamed kindly at them all.

Until now, I had become used to juggling my life around the hospital and the girls, their crises and – sometimes - their good company. When each holiday came around, Mama Mary and I sighed with relief, thankful that we had survived another term. The girls were always excited to be going home but would nevertheless be sorry to leave me all on my own! Therefore they were very pleased the next holiday when the ten boys smilingly turned up with their odd bits of pathetic belongings, hoping to sleep in the hostel for the holidays.

"Now you won't be lonely!" the girls comforted me.

It would be some time yet, but those ten little boys were there when I was arrested, standing in a row outside my house, looking unbelieving - shocked and silent. One of them, seeing the policeman with a gun, ran off to get his bow and arrows to shoot him and had to be persuaded it was not a good idea. But I'm getting ahead of myself.

On My Own

Over the months, anti-British propaganda on Uganda Radio moved up a notch. David, with the responsibility of his family, felt the weight of it far more than the rest of us. He appealed for advice to our District

Commissioner, Mr Owor, our neighbour and a regular member of the church. On David's mind were questions like 'Should we all get out? Or should David just take Rosemary and the boys to safety over the border and come back to Amudat alone?'

Mr Owor advised, "Stay for now. I'll let you know when you need to get out. Be ready at a moment's notice."

We all packed 'flee bags' - torch, water etc - so we could escape instantly to the nearby hills on the Kenyan border. We never had to use the flee bags, but once Mr Owor tipped David off and we all bundled into the Land Rover and headed for Kenya (the back way). We stayed at the top of the escarpment at Nasakol, the BCMS School, and tried to keep our minds occupied. Di remembers being press-ganged into teaching science lessons with no text books! We were away a whole month.

After our return to Amudat, Radio Uganda continued to attack the British and especially British missionaries. They accused us of being spies, and I could feel some people's attitude towards us changing, although not the people who knew us well. David was being tailed wherever he went by a Special Branch 'minder' which he found very unsettling although he joked about it a lot. Rosemary began getting fevers, reminding us of the fevers Peter Cox used to have.

Eventually, the Websters felt they had no choice but to move on.

"Who would be willing to come to Uganda at a time like this?" we asked ourselves.

Miraculously, someone *was* willing! John and Libby Wattis, a young couple without any children, were looking around for God's plan for them for the next two years. No visas were being issued to British missionaries but, amazingly, they were given one.

Doctor Webster and his family left Amudat in June, 1973 with regret on their parts and tears on ours. Six months later, they returned to East Africa, to Marsabit Hospital in Kenya, which had been their original destination when they had set out six years earlier.

One problem was that Dr. Wattis couldn't come immediately. Di finished her year at Amudat and returned to work in London; so I was the only missionary left. The mission asked Anne Wright (the

Karamoja Mothers' Union Worker) to move fifty miles to keep me company. I had met Anne when I was on UK leave and I liked her. She was sensible and unflappable. She also enjoyed cooking, and when she moved to Amudat, she gave me delicious lunches every day! We heard on the news that two British men had been arrested – one for 'hoarding' cooking oil and the other, a journalist, for calling Amin a 'village pumpkin' in an article! I thanked the Lord for Anne's company.

We still had no doctor so Keith Knox, realising our predicament, offered to come back to fill in the gap till Dr. Wattis arrived. By now, Keith had just passed his medical exams but postponed his registration as a doctor in order to come immediately. Of course, the girls were thrilled and began embroidering little cloths for him with the words 'Kith, I love you!'

It felt strange being the longest standing missionary in Amudat and in charge of the hospital; so I wasn't surprised when someone brought the message to the hospital that I was wanted at a meeting. I left the keys with Justus and followed the messenger in the blazing sun across the main road and past the road block to a circle of men sitting on benches under a shady tree. The NCO in charge of Amudat was there, called Sergeant Nyoka, meaning 'Snake', and so was the governor. I recognised faces I knew from the schools: local shopkeepers and elders. I wondered what we were going to discuss.

I was shocked when I discovered it was me under scrutiny. I had to stand there on my own in front of all these seated men and answer a barrage of questions.

"Why do junior dressers administer injections? Why do you refuse to see patients? Why don't you give your patients more food? You should give mothers' dried milk for their babies!"

I sensed the antagonism of the men staring at me. They seemed to be enjoying seeing a white woman in a vulnerable position. I felt an overwhelming fear well up inside me. Then I sensed God taking over and giving me the right words to answer in a convincing manner. In the end, all the men were won over and the bad atmosphere just melted away. I didn't know it then but a year later, Sergeant Snake would help to arrest me.

Arrested!

I hadn't been too worried when I saw two Land Rovers parking under the hospital tree. But I was puzzled when I recognised our Chief of Police getting out together with the Governor, Sergeant Snake, and seven others in uniform! They demanded to search my house, took my passport and looked at some recent letters. Then they escorted me to the hospital and we all crowded into the doctor's office. The governor began to speak, riffling through my passport. At this point, fear rose up inside me, almost choking me. My legs began to give way and I propped myself against a table. I knew he was about to say something devastating, and he did.

"You must come away with us."

I found no words. I couldn't even think. I heard Anne bravely arguing with him in her Yorkshire accent.

"What has she done?"

"Confusing religions," he said.

"Well then, if you're going to arrest her, you might as well arrest the lot of us. She's done no more to confuse religions than the rest of us have!"

"It's nothing to do with you; you just get out and stop interfering."

John Wattis tried to reason with them. It was useless. Sergeant Snake held out his hand showing the order to arrest me, and he refused to say where they were taking me.

With the help of Anne and Libby, I changed out of uniform and packed a suitcase. We remembered to pack a Bible and my daily reading notes, but somehow I also put in a pair of curtains!

I was squeezed into the Land Rover between two burly policewomen. The staff and some of the patients stood watching in silence. I gave them a scared smile and waved. There was no response, just angry, embarrassed looks. Only John Wattis stepped forward with a white, shocked face and shook my hand in silence.

"What are you accused of?" asked the police driver chattily above the rattles of the rutted road.

"Confusing religions," I answered.

"And what else?"

"Nothing at all."

"You can't be arrested just for that; you must have done something else."

"I haven't," I protested, "and I haven't even confused religions."

I watched the familiar landscape disappear rapidly past us. I saw Cholol, a knoll where I often took a Land Rover full of excited girls for picnics and letting off steam in the dry riverbed. I gazed up at Kadam Mountain whose rugged outline brought to mind the psalm I had memorised as a child: "I will lift up my eyes to the hills. Where does my help come from? My help comes from the LORD!"

"Help, Lord!" I silently cried out, "I may never see all this again," and I tried not to cry.

I reminded myself that the Lord was helping already. Anne had abandoned the Mothers' Union course she was preparing to run, had jumped into her car and was following us - as close behind our cloud of dust as she could. But we were driving faster than Anne's little car could manage, and Anne lost us when we detoured to a small town to send radio messages.

I knew the pastor there, Rev. Peter Lomongin, so I asked a policeman to call him. He arrived, speechless with anger. I explained what was happening and he rushed home and gathered his family together to pray for me. (I didn't know that till later, of course. Nor did I know that John and Libby Wattis had leapt into the hospital Land Rover, driven through 'the back door' into Kenya and telephoned BCMS headquarters in UK.)

While the pastor and his family were praying for us we drove on to Moroto where Anne caught up with us again just as the sun was going down. Next morning, Anne was joined in the car with another of our missionaries, Sylvia Barton. My spirits rose every time the two of them popped up wherever we stopped!

Even my police guards were impressed and one of them exclaimed, "Faithful friends!"

We drove on in the heat for mile after mile. Once we stopped for 'army rations' - a tin of corned beef and dry biscuits - which they ate by attacking the meat with a hard biscuit. I was offered some too. I forced myself to eat, but I had no appetite.

Eventually we arrived in Kampala and drove through road after road to the central police station. The guards led me down some steep steps to the cells. The air smelt stale, lacking oxygen. The warders told me to wait while they barked orders to prisoners and juggled them around. They unlocked one cell, and a horrible stench wafted out as ten men were hustled into a different cell and I was locked in the emptied one. I stood there, horrified.

I remember that I couldn't pray – just... "Jesus, Jesus."

A bare bulb and a dirty skylight near the ceiling showed up the black walls, scrawled with years of graffiti. Around my feet was rubbish – tin plates with dried-on food, empty bottles, worn out shoes and dirty rags. In a corner was the sink and, sunken into the floor, the toilet.

I sat on my case wondering what would happen next. Each time the key rattled in the lock to let someone in, my heart thumped wildly. I remembered the nightmares I used to have, even during my nurse's training - that a burglar was in my room!

My friends would say, "What will you do when you are a missionary and you don't have us to run to?"

I was to learn that the God who called me was right there with me, even in that cell.

A warder peered through the bars and asked, "What did you do?"

I gave my usual reply and then, as he began to move away, I managed to blurt out, "Please, may I have a bed?"

"I'm sorry, but we have no beds," he replied politely.

"But I can't sleep here," I choked. "I'm afraid... I'm afraid of bedbugs and rats."

Looking embarrassed, he walked away. I felt more frightened and more alone than ever before. That was when I remembered that in the Bible, St. Paul and Silas sang psalms when they were imprisoned.

"Ruth, try singing the 23rd Psalm," I told myself.

I took a shaky breath and started to sing, "The Lord's my Shepherd"... but failed to get out any more than a croak and burst into tears.

The inspector I had met at the front desk came and looked through the bars. He had a rough, rugged, dark complexion, but he said in a polite, gentle voice, "We have received your complaint, but we are sorry we cannot help you; we have no beds."

After all that had happened so far, the fact that I had to sleep on boards was a comparatively small matter, but I burst into tears again.

Troubled, the inspector asked, "Do you have any friends in the city?"

I knew Anne Wright must be in Kampala by now, but I did not know where to find her.

"I'll phone the British Consul for you," he decided.

Anne had already been to the Consulate, so they were aware that a British nurse from a remote mission hospital had been arrested.

"Er, what is this Bible Churchman's Missionary Society?" the official had asked Anne, looking embarrassed. "What... er... sect are you?"

He was visibly relieved to discover that we were not some strange sect that he had to get out of a scrape but members of the Church of Uganda with Archbishop Janani Luwuum to represent us.

Soon there was a rattle of keys and my heart thumped. The warder brought in the British Consul, laden down with a mattress, food and clean, cool water. I don't know what he expected - perhaps an indignant UK citizen, angrily demanding justice and British protection. Nothing was further from my mind. I must have looked a scared, scruffy specimen, standing five feet and half an inch high, with my profession obvious from the fob watch hanging like a medal on my grubby dress.

When he had gone, I shakily ate one of the jam tarts his wife had sent and I drank the clean water. Then, as it was the sort of time people in normal situations go to bed, I prepared to do the same. I was given permission to cover the bars with a towel, had a 'bath' and put on some trousers. I wrapped myself, my money and my fob watch in a blanket, put a torch nearby ready for an emergency, and closed my eyes.

I slept restlessly, under the glare of the electric light bulb, wondering what awaited me the next day: Deportation? Release? A military prison? Or was it something worse?

I thought of my parents sleeping comfortably at home.

I prayed, "Oh Lord, may my parents not know where their troublesome daughter is until this is over."

Janani Luwuum

I woke at four in the morning, the electric light still burning, and I knew I wouldn't get back to sleep. I decided to read the Bible verses chosen for that morning in my Scripture Union notes. I knew that the Bible is God speaking to us, and I had experienced that in some measure over the years. But this morning I needed something very special.

"God," I said, "you've got to speak to me today; I don't know what I'll do if my set reading is something just ordinary. So, please, speak to me now!"

I opened up my Bible, in fear and trembling. Would God speak? The morning reading was Acts chapter 12 verses 1 to 11. I began to read...

"It was about this time that King Herod arrested some who belonged to the church..."

I stopped in amazement, tears pouring down my cheeks. The day's reading was especially for me! I felt ashamed of myself that I had ever doubted God. I read on to verse 5.

"...so Peter was kept in prison, but the church was earnestly praying to God for him..."

I felt that God was right there in my cell, comforting me and telling me that many people were praying for me. Little did I know how many! Even in the UK people were praying for me; one Bible College prayed all night.

When daylight seeped through the grimy skylight, I asked for a broom and swept up all the mess – shoes, old newspapers, stale food. Someone brought me some food which I forced myself to eat, thinking, "Who knows when I'll be given any more."

There was another rattle of keys, the door opened and I saw Anne and Sylvia's horrified faces! They told me how they had lost track of me in Kampala and had searched and searched, contacting the British Consul and the archbishop.

After they had left, the inspector brought in someone else and in a tone of deep respect said, "Here's the archbishop to see you!"

A gentle voice said, "Ruth, I'm Janani Luwuum!"

He hugged me. Tears overflowed again.

"Don't worry, you're sure to be deported today," he assured me.

He sat on the bed board and chatted and prayed for me. I felt calmer now! After about half-an-hour he left, and once again they slammed the door shut and locked me in.

I waited and waited, sitting on my case expecting someone to take me to the airport. I lay on the board... I read a book... I read my Bible. I jumped up every time someone looked through the bars or rattled the lock. The hours passed agonisingly as I waited for something to happen. I caught a very faint glimmer of what it must be like for Christians in a communist prison: the loneliness, the uncertainty, the fear. Those prisoners had no friends as I had who were doing their utmost to obtain my release. So I prayed for those unknown people.

I thought about Amudat people and prayed for them. I prayed for all the girls who would have come home from school to discover I had gone. I prayed for Anne, Sylvia and the others who were so kind and concerned and trying to cheer me up.

Anne and Sylvia were allowed in the cell again later that day, and they brought me some gifts from others – a rose in a tiny bottle of water and some chocolate, even though chocolate was unheard of since the deterioration of Uganda's economy. Then - another night in the cell!

As soon as I awoke, I picked up my Bible, eager to hear God speak to me again. The set verses for the day were from the same chapter as the day before – Acts chapter 12. They described how Peter was miraculously released from prison by an angel. Then he made his way to the home of some Christian friends; but when he knocked at the door, the servant-girl Rhoda was so excited that she ran back to tell everyone and forgot to open the door!

At this point, the door of my cell rattled and I leapt up. Was it an angel?

A policeman gruffly told me to follow him. I followed him for what seemed a long, long way. I can remember going up some stairs

49

and through numerous locked doors, and as I went, I gulped in clean air – so sweet!

Behind the many locked doors sat the special branch detective at a desk with others around him.

He asked me the question they all asked: "What did you do?"

I gave the same reply and added, "It's all in the letter which the governor sent you."

"But we haven't located the officer who brought you, so we haven't read it yet. Who arrested you?"

"Twelve officials came in two Land Rovers to arrest me," I replied.

"Twelve men to arrest you!" they laughed incredulously, looking me up and down. "You had better tell us all about it. Did you quarrel with someone? Do you have any enemies?"

I shook my head.

"Be careful how you answer that question," one warned. "It's important."

"I have no enemies," I repeated.

They asked me to write a full report of everything that had happened. I was left in the room with one special police officer, some paper and a pen. We were a few floors up and I looked longingly through the window. The scene looked so inviting - flowering trees in the garden down below - and beyond, a lovely tropical town with women walking along looked so graceful in their brightly coloured Ugandan costumes. The air smelt so sweet after the foetid smell of the cell. I took deep breaths and settled down to writing.

Pen in hand, I asked myself, "Do I have an enemy?

I asked the policewoman, "If I do have an enemy and give her name, could she get into trouble?"

"Yes, of course," she replied.

"Then how can I mention a name?"

"But someone is making you suffer," she objected.

"But I'm a Christian trying to show God's love."

She looked puzzled and repeated, "Look what you are suffering."

"But Jesus suffered and died for me on the cross..." I began.

Suddenly the door opened and our conversation ended abruptly - my one and only bit of 'witnessing' about my faith. I had often read about Christians in dire situations, and they always seemed to find opportunities to witness. But I couldn't even be like Paul and Silas and sing psalms!

I had to stand in front of the special branch detective again. He scanned through what I had written. He still seemed unsure and puzzled.

"You can go back to your cell now," he instructed.

I had so enjoyed the clean air that the thought of going back to that cell was horrifying.

"Do I *have* to go back to the cell?" I asked.

"Why, don't you like it?"

"It smells," I replied.

He looked embarrassed, hesitated, then said, "Wait here a minute."

I waited for a whole hour but not complaining – anything was better than the dreadful smell in the cell.

He came back saying, "You are still under arrest, but I have arranged for you to go to the archbishop - still under arrest, you understand. You must not to move out of the house. Is that understood?"

I nodded vehemently and thanked him sincerely. Then I was shown into a luxury car and driven in style to Archbishop Janani Luwuum's home on Mengo Hill. The guard knocked at the door.

The archbishop and his secretary, another Sylvia, welcomed me with great jubilation and enveloping hugs.

"We have just been reading the Bible passage for today," they laughed, "and we were nearly like Rhoda, not opening the door!"

Even though I was under house arrest, the relief was enormous. The archbishop put me in his secretary's house and reinforced what I had been told - not to move out of the door. I had no objection to that! It was great that Anne and Sylvia stayed there with me. I was content to sit around all day, revelling in the cleanliness, sweet air and peace. The archbishop, serene and cheerful, popped in from time to time to see me. What an amazing man! At that time I knew so little about what he was busy doing, but I now know he was the one to whom everyone turned in those terrible days whenever there was trouble or someone was missing. He was the angel!

Suddenly, on the third day, the archbishop burst into the room saying, "Have you heard the news? You are free! I've seen Idi Amin myself and he says you have done nothing wrong. You may go back to Amudat and forget the whole affair!"

Return to Amudat

Next morning we did just that. We said emotional goodbyes to the archbishop, and the three of us set off in Anne's car on the long journey home. We dropped Sylvia off in Moroto. There in her driveway, we had an impromptu praise meeting with people who quickly gathered as the news spread. We were excited and eager to tell everyone how God had answered our prayers and had become nearer to each one of us.

Then the last seventy miles to Amudat... I was apprehensive and voiced it to Anne. There had been no way of letting anyone know what was happening, so would the girls and boys think that I had done something bad? Perhaps no one would want to shake hands with me!

As we drew near to our houses, Anne kept pressing the car horn. *Toot... toot... toot.* Finally we stopped at the doctor's house. John and Libby rushed out and hugged us tearfully.

I reached the kitchen doorway and heard children's voices, and before I could turn around, five little girls shot at me like bullets, knocking me flat on the floor. We lay in a heap, crying and laughing. I found a wall to lean against for the next onslaught. Girls, women and their children flung themselves at me - touching me, hugging me. We all cried unashamedly.

Why had I dared to doubt them?

That evening, all the hospital staff, together with the older girls, met in the doctor's house to hear what had happened in that long, long week.

"We want to know every detail," they said.

Anne and I told the story of how God had been faithful to us, how we had experienced His close presence all the time, and how He had spoken to us through different parts of the Bible.

At the end Justus said, "Tonight we have had a living Bible Study. Many passages in the Bible have come alive to us."

Rev. Daudi added, "We have not yet experienced persecution here, but it may come to us. We have seen for ourselves that God can work wonders and this will give us courage."

Someone called out, "Let's sing..."

Yesterday, today, forever, Jesus is the same,

All may change, but Jesus never,

Glory to His name.

We sang it in Pokot, then Swahili, then English.

The first thing I did next morning was to wander round the shops in our main street, being welcomed back and shaking hands with everyone. I drank four cups of sweet tea with the dressers' wives and with some of the shopkeepers.

More than one Muslim shopkeeper said, "Sister Ruth, we prayed for you when you were taken away. We prayed to Allah for you."

Then I made my way to the hospital, avoiding the road-block. The veranda was crowded as usual with patients and relatives. One old Pokot elder saw me, came over and shook hands. He was wearing the usual mud headdress with an ostrich feather waving at the top. He was wearing shorts with his shuka flung over his back. Like most Pokot men, he had a hole in his lower lip, plugged with a piece of ivory, and he was chewing the inevitable tobacco.

He held my hand and sprayed it with tobacco-stained spit, saying, "Chepcoggis, we prayed to Tororut for you; we prayed in our Pokot way."

That's the only time I've been 'kissed' in this way! The other men standing around nodded and hummed in agreement.

"Owei," they said.

Everyone at the hospital thought it would be good for me to go away for a few days' rest to Kenya. So once more I set off, this time in the hospital Land Rover, using the 'back door' into Kenya, avoiding roadblocks.

Timothy and Mary had already been transferred from Amudat

and were now looking after a church in Kitale (the nearest big town to the Ugandan border). When I rolled up in the Land Rover, they were ecstatic.

Mary kept saying, "Don't go back, msichana wangu (my girl). It's not safe for you."

I laughed off her arguments and told her, "But it's all safe now! The archbishop has assured us it can't possibly happen again. Anyway, I can't leave the girls yet and the hospital needs me..."

So after three days of cosseting, I bumped my way back to Amudat. I felt refreshed and was looking forward to the future and all our plans for the hospital and the hostel. At the weekend the girls and I cut out blue school uniforms, ready for them to hand-sew the next week.

Farewell Uganda

About ten days later, I was on the veranda at the hospital, dressing tropical ulcers. I looked up and saw the two policewomen walking towards me, complete with guns. They stopped the other side of the low veranda wall.

I thought to myself, "That's interesting; they've come to try out our medicine!"

I smiled a welcome.

One said, "Hello, Luth; we've come to take you again!"

I couldn't believe my ears; then I saw the police Land Rover with our police officer inside. Yes, those were the orders – he had the radio message in his hand.

We followed the same routine as before. Back at my house, Anne and Libby packed a suitcase while I sat stunned. The news must have spread rapidly to the school because all the girls and boys had left their lessons and were standing there in silence. I dared not even glance at them.

I heard the policewoman say, "Look at that boy; he is crying!"

I stared rigidly ahead. Anne was as strong as ever and she asked the police if I could travel in her tiny car. Surprisingly they agreed, on condition that we squeezed the two heavy policewomen in the back (plus Kalashnikovs). As we drove away, I glanced back at the town where ten years of my life had been spent. Then the mountain, Kadam, loomed large to my left, and I knew deep down inside me that this time I would not be coming back nor see its beautiful rugged shape again.

Suddenly we saw a warthog trotting rapidly across the road, and the policewomen called Anne to stop so that they could shoot it.

But Anne was soft about animals and answered shortly, "No, I won't! I'm not stopping for you to shoot innocent animals."

I whispered, "Anne, be careful!"

But they just accepted it. I wondered where they would have put the dead warthog. The car boot was chock-a-block.

That night was again spent under guard in the same town as before. But this time it was made easier by another of Anne's requests being granted - that I might spend the night in Sylvia's house (with a guard, of course, to make sure I didn't escape!)

The guard made himself comfortable in the sitting room for the night. Very early next morning he was puzzled to see a lot of people creeping silently into the house. I was having a good sleep when Anne woke me.

"Ruth, get up; there are about thirty visitors for you!"

The Christians of Moroto had come to pray with me. I walked into the sitting room and was overwhelmed to see it packed! The pastor prayed for me and read some encouraging verses from the Bible. Then he announced that we would sing the hymn 'God be with you till we meet again' and, as we sang, everyone was to file past me and shake my hand. The haunting tune was very emotional and some of them broke down - what could you expect?

We were all hugging and weeping when Pastor Joram said, "Stop all this! The police are waiting to leave."

We spent another day bumping along the hot dusty roads behind the police Land Rover. Towards evening we arrived in the capital, Kampala. I was fearful we were being led to the notorious Military Base. But no, we stopped at an insignificant-looking building where an officer of the Special Branch Police was expecting us. He began by apologising.

"This was not how Ugandans behave but it's the fault of the present regime. Please, don't think badly about us."

He handed me a deportation order together with a ticket to England for a flight leaving in just over two hours. What a relief! Anne drove me on to Entebbe Airport. The police Land Rover which we had been following all the way from Amudat seemed to have disappeared - together with my suitcase! I couldn't care less at that moment. Anne tipped out the contents of her purse for me. I was joined by an Asian man and a C.M.S. missionary, John Holden, who were being deported on the same flight. The Special Branch policeman, still apologising, insisted in carrying my shoulder bag across the tarmac and, as I stepped onto the gangway of the plane, he shook hands with me, still apologising.

I climbed up the steps of the Boeing 707 and sank into the plush seats, feeling very grubby. As it took off, I fell asleep, and when I woke up, I found I was sitting next to John Holden. He told me how worried he was about his children. They were at a boarding school in Kenya – St Andrew's, Turi.

"They are so young," he told me. "I would hate them to hear about all this from the newspapers or something."

After about an hour the plane touched down at Nairobi Airport, and we were all escorted into the Transit Lounge. I wondered if the news had been phoned through that I'd been deported and if there was someone at the airport looking for me. I spied an airport official and went to ask if I could go out and look. Reluctantly, he let me out of a side door.

Immediately Peter Cox flashed past.

"Peter!" I shouted.

He whirled around, bounded towards me and hugged me.

"What's happened? I've just had coffee with your archbishop; he's here in Nairobi on church business. He asked me to tell the Mission that you could never ever be put in prison again. Then I got this phone call - you've been deported!?"

Breathlessly, I tried to explain. Then I hurried on because I had two things on my mind.

"Please, send a telegram to my parents in South Africa."

"What shall I say?"

After some hesitation, I replied, "Put 'Deported from Uganda to England', and you'd better add 'Halleluya' just so they'd know I'm okay."

56

I then told Peter about John Holden and his worry about his children. Peter said, "Tell him I'll go straight to Turi and explain to his children myself that their Daddy is safe in England."

He set off the hundred or so miles to Turi, and I dodged back through the side door into the Transit Lounge... "Just time to phone Pru..." I muttered to myself.

I knew my friend Pru was in Nairobi. All she could say was, "Oh Ruth, oh Ruth!"

Then I heard the announcement to board and I ran back just in time to board the plane. John Holden breathed a huge sigh of relief at my news.

Early the next morning we both arrived, dishevelled and disorientated, at Heathrow Airport. We quietly slipped into Britain with no publicity. At the time, two British men were in prison in Uganda, sentenced to death - the journalist who had called Amin a 'village pumpkin' and the man accused of hoarding cooking oil. The British Government were anxious not to antagonise Amin more than necessary.

Alan Neech, the BCMS General Secretary, met us and took us to CMS House and to our different Mission offices. John Holden and I never met again.

There was someone one else I would never see again although I had no way of knowing it at the time; Archbishop Janani Luwuum would be murdered a few years later for doing much the same as he did for me many times over.

Missionary Aviation Fellowship plane touches down at Amudat

Young ladies, dressed for a dance

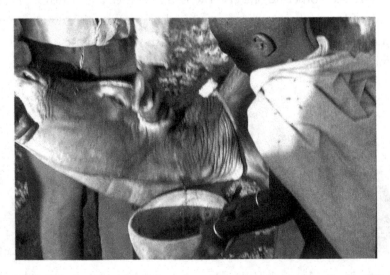

Daily local diet – blood from jugular vein of a cow in the herd"

flooded Amudat river

Ruth holding her Deportation order

Dear God, Am I Dreaming?

Friday, 6ᵗʰ June 1975

11 am: Dear God, am I dreaming or am I really in London, walking down Oxford Street? It's only twenty-four hours since I was bumping along in Anne's little car. The tropical sun was beating down, sticking my clean dress to the seat. With those 'sylph-like' policewomen in the back, it was like an oven. Now my clean dress is dusty and crumpled and stained. Anne's comb is still in my bag and I have some money in an envelope to buy a change of clothes.

12 noon: I'm being taken into Oxford Street shops now; crowds of people are milling around me of all colours and nationalities. Lord, was it only yesterday that I had that dreadful farewell with the Moroto Christians? I'm sorry I broke down. It was because Margaret burst into tears and because of the hymn 'God be with you till we meet again.' I couldn't even thank them as I wanted to. They were so concerned, so loving, so full of pain - I suppose they will get over it. So will I but not yet.

2 pm: I haven't started to feel yet, Father; my heart has gone into neutral gear. I can hear myself chatting, laughing, and parading my new clothes through the BCMS offices. But inside I'm not here at all; I'm there in Amudat. What are they doing now? Have they used up the food I left in the fridge? I didn't finish writing out that list. Did I give Chepich her treatment, or didn't I? At least the girls' uniforms were all cut out; I hope they will be able to sew them by hand. I don't suppose I'll ever hear, will I Lord?

5 pm: Goodness me! Look at the time! Everyone wants to go home, and I'm holding them up. Audrey has invited me to her flat for the night. Thank you Lord, for Your care of me!

9 pm: I suddenly remembered, Lord, that it's my friend Margaret's wedding tomorrow in St. Margaret's, Westminster. She posted me an invitation to Amudat for a joke! I blurted out, "I'll be in time for Margaret's wedding at Westminster tomorrow!" Audrey was horrified: "You can't go looking like that!" She rushed out to confer with friends and neighbours while I fell into bed. I wonder what Audrey's doing.

Saturday, 7th June

10.30 am: Thank you, Lord, that I slept like a log last night, but am I dreaming – or am I really sitting on this bus? Was that really my reflection I gazed at in Audrey's mirror? I saw a small, thin woman dressed up for a wedding. She was wearing a long, floral dress, hastily shortened, lent by Audrey's friend across the corridor. Her hair looked good; someone had set it after breakfast. It must have been me because Audrey's shoes fit me so well and the girl-next-door's handbag matches. They had all trouped with me to the bus stop and said, "Ask the bus driver to put you off at Westminster."

11.30 am: It is so soothing, Lord, sitting here in church, waiting for the wedding. The music from this vast organ sounds heavenly; the girls in Amudat sing beautifully too. Some people might call them raucous but their enthusiastic singing sounded to me as heavenly as this organ. Everyone looks so smart. Thank you, Lord, that no one knows that everything I'm wearing is borrowed. I'm glad they didn't see me yesterday when I arrived at Heathrow - like a waif!

4 pm: We've just had that amazing reception, Lord, and all that food! It was funny when they began introducing me, pushing me from one guest to another. "Do meet Ruth. She has just been deported by Idi Amin; she was a prisoner in Uganda." Cultured tones gave suitable replies. The children stared, wide-eyed. I caused more of a sensation than the bride!

9 pm: I'm snuggling down now in a comfortable bed after that hectic day. But, dear Lord Jesus, why is your Word not alive to me now as it was in that cell? I was so excited then to discover that you do speak to your children. It was an amazing experience to find that the Scripture Union reading for that very day was about Peter in prison and his miraculous escape. God, did You arrange that reading especially for me? I think so. Then You got me out of that cell just as miraculously but through a different sort of angel: Archbishop Janani Luwuum!

Anne and Sylvia's reading was spot-on too – all about Paul's weaknesses. You knew how weak and weepy I was - not a bit like one of your brave Christian soldiers; more like a quivering jelly! I'm so sorry. Do you remember, Lord, I couldn't sing psalms, not even one note? But those Bible verses penetrated right down inside me and gave me peace, like lotion on my scratches. Thank you, Lord.

Thank you too, Lord, for that bonus – letting me go back to Amudat for those precious two weeks. You wanted me to see the joy which my friends felt when I came back to them. You wanted me to feel the love which they have for me. I had been so worried they might believe I had done something wrong; now I know it's alright. Thank You, Lord, again and again...

But, Father, I find it hard to thank You for the situation in Amudat now. You know that the doctor leaves soon and the senior dresser will have too much responsibility, and what about Rev. Daudi, the shopkeeper? He'll miss our encouragement in these crazy times. What about the girls and boys?

Yes, I know there is a church now and thank you for that. I know that there are fine Christians, in spite of my many mistakes, and there are promising younger ones coming along. I'm not complaining; it's just that I left so suddenly. May Your will be done. Bless them, Father, as they carry on Your work there in Jesus' name. AMEN.

God Meant it for Good!

After a weekend in London, I headed north for Yorkshire. On my last UK leave, Keith Knox, the young medical student, had introduced me to Leonard and Winifred Webster at Oakwood Farm in Knaresborough, North Yorkshire. They and their three boys had made me very, very welcome, and Oakwood Farm had become a home from home. I had helped with an English harvest and driven a machine called a 'woofler'!

So as soon as Winifred heard the news that I had been deported, she phoned.

"When are you coming home?" she asked.

So Oakwood Farm seemed the natural place to make a bee-line for.

Even though the government was trying to hush everything up, members of the press somehow sniffed out the news. They contacted people with the same surname as mine including Dad's brother, Uncle Eddie. Sensibly he told them he didn't know anything about it and put the phone down. He thought this a huge joke and phoned me at the farm to regale me with it. Leonard and Winifred decided I should never answer the phone. Secretly I was a little disappointed that I hadn't made a media splash!

I settled down quietly at Oakwood Farm. It was June, soft fruit was ripening and the weather was warm. One day, seeing me wandering aimlessly around, Winifred handed me a basket and said, "Pick us some gooseberries!"

I drifted to the gooseberry patch and peacefully filled it with fruit, all the time thinking about Amudat, the arrests and how God had felt so close to me; but since then it had felt as if the phoneline to God had been cut off.

While picking gooseberries, I recalled my Bible readings of the last few days and it dawned on me that that God was still speaking to me. I was reading from the book of Genesis about Joseph. His brothers had sold Joseph and he had become a slave in Egypt, but he had ended up as Egypt's Minister of Food during a long famine. His brothers came looking for food and when they discovered that the Very Important Man was Joseph they were terrified. He had comforted them saying, "God meant it for good."

It seemed that there in the gooseberry bushes God Himself was reminding me that He meant the entire past few weeks' trauma for good.

I dripped tears into the gooseberries asking God, "How can this be true?"

We had gooseberry pie for tea!

About two weeks after my arrival, I wandered into the lounge at the farm to a chorus of "You're famous; you've been on telly!" My deportation had been a main item on the ITV News but I never saw it! However, I did make the front page of the Daily Telegraph! The news had been released after the two British men imprisoned in Uganda had been freed. Amin had insisted that a Member of the House of Lords visit him to beg for clemency, and he sat in a tent with a very low entrance so that he had the satisfaction of seeing a British Peer approach him on his knees!

I was keen to tell everyone the amazing things that God had done for me, and BCMS arranged for me to visit the many supporting churches which I had collected over the previous ten years. These were scattered throughout England – from Ditton in Kent and Wandsworth in London to St Helen's, Stapleford, where my brother Alan had been a curate. Of course, I had links in Blackpool: Christ Church, where my parents had married, and Bispham, where our cousins had grown up. Further north still I had a village church near Hull; another in Normanton, near Leeds; and finally a cluster of five village churches near Northallerton led by an energetic vicar called Geoff Wood. These all kept me busy. Everyone was very loving and lifelong friendships cemented.

Letters kept arriving at the farm from friends and even from people I didn't know. One letter was very touching; I opened it to find a note from two boys aged nine and eleven, which read something like this: "We heard about your being imprisoned and we prayed for you. We are glad you are safe now. We emptied our money boxes so please will you buy yourself a dress or something. Love from Quentin and Simon." A postal order for £1.60p was enclosed, and I bought a blouse at Knaresborough Market!

That sort of thing helped. I'm not naturally an early bird, but I was waking up before six every morning. Winifred would come down to the snug farmhouse kitchen, with its warm Aga, surprised to find me already there, sipping tea. Then one eyelid started to twitch annoyingly and I couldn't stop it.

Winifred would jokingly tell it, "Stop that! Stop twitching!" but it didn't listen.

The summer of 1975 was a very hot one. I helped with young peoples' camps and the young people at Gracious Street Methodist Church in Knaresborough. On Sundays, with some of the young people, we would take Sunday afternoon services at Knaresborough Hospital and an old folks' home. The youth leaders, Andy Wheeler and Bob Drew, were both teachers and gifted musicians and led an amazing youth choir with Keith Knox, the very same crazy young doctor who had helped us out in Amudat!

At the end of the summer, my eyelid still twitching, I flew to South Africa to see my family – and, as my headmaster had predicted over twenty years earlier, I *did* make the newspaper headlines! "DURBAN GIRL'S BRUSH WITH AMIN," the Daily News announced in huge letters on the front page above my photograph! The South African Broadcasting Corporation asked me for an interview on a magazine programme which went out all over South Africa. So I had my bit of fame!

As soon as I was reunited with my parents, they told me their side of the story. In my prison cell, I had prayed that my parents wouldn't hear about what was happening until it was all over and I was safe again. After I had been released, I decided I had better tell them everything. I had filled five blue air-letters with a blow-by-blow account and had posted them in Kenya.

Mother said, "When those five aerogrammes arrived, we were on holiday, you know. Mark picked them up and put them with the rest of the post, thinking that you were a bit over the top with your letter writing!"

My father chipped in, "So we hadn't even read your five letters when the telegram arrived."

"DEPORTED FROM UGANDA TO UK ALLELUIA." My mother sobbed.

"Mark rang at once," Dad continued. "We rushed home, left everything in the car, dashed into the house and read your five air-letters. You should have seen your mother crying!"

I thanked God that He had answered my cry in the cell and that they knew I was safe before they read the letters. In spite of how upset my mother was, she and Dad never hinted that I should look for a less exciting job; I wonder if they thought it.

In Durban, there was a flurry of church meetings and reunions. Then I flew to Cape Town to visit Alan and Marian who had moved there to work for The Bible Society. They arranged another flurry of meetings for me, and their daughter Ann, now a tall schoolgirl, invited me to speak at her school Christian Union.

Now everyone was asking me, "What will you do next, Ruth?"

I had no answer. Then my eyelid stopped twitching, and I began to ask myself the same question: "What next, Ruth?"

One of my friends sang to me, "One step at a time, Lord Jesus; that's all I'm asking from you!"

The first step was obvious: return to the UK. Back in Knaresborough, one hot summer day, I was walking with Andy along the High Street, when we saw a tall old house with a 'For Sale' notice.

Andy mused, "Wouldn't it be good if we four - you, Keith, Bob and I - joined forces and bought that house. It's so near the church!"

"It would certainly be good for the youth work," I agreed. "Let's see if there's anyone in."

We knocked on the door. An old lady opened the door and invited us in. The first thing we noticed was a row of twelve double coat-hooks in the hall.

We looked at each other and nodded, "That's a good sign!"

I pictured those coat-hooks laden with the young people's jackets. She showed us seven bedrooms and three cellars. Eventually, to the alarm of all our friends, the four of us bought it – Keith, Andy, Bob and I - me on the property ladder with three young men in their twenties, all involved with the youth work and choir!

Our friends shook their heads at the mad venture. Sounded crazy! It *was* crazy because we were all unsure about our futures and all hoping to go somewhere in 'the four quarters' of the globe. Keith for instance, was prayerfully turning over in his mind whether God was calling him back to Amudat. We called the house 'Four Quarters'.

Just before Christmas, I moved from Oakwood Farm into Four Quarters with very little to put in it. The previous owner had moved to a much smaller place and had left the house far from empty so I had a bed and even some furniture. Friends gave us stuff and I bought bedding in a charity shop. I became a temporary Staff Nurse at a hospital near Knaresborough, while considering the all-important "What next?"

The four of us unanimously agreed that we needed 'paying guests' to help us pay off the loan. We all agreed that they must be Christians, to keep the right ethos. So we were puzzled when we all felt it was right to accept as our first 'paying guest' a student nurse who was not a Christian.

Debi was a fledgling nurse to whom I had taught the mysteries of giving injections on a very thin, game lady. Debi had told me (over a bed bath) that she wasn't a Christian but thought it was 'quite sweet'! It was only a few weeks after Debi joined us that she tasted how 'sweet' it is and began her own Christian journey. She became the mainstay of Four Quarters and hospitable to a fault as Four Quarters became the hub of church youth activities. I introduced Debi to my Chocolate Brownie recipe and it became the tradition of Four Quarters – so easy to make; just throw everything in, beat and bake!

Chocolate Brownies were a great hit with the other 'Three Quarters' especially Keith Knox. By the spring of 1976 Keith had decided that God was calling him back to Amudat. A large crowd waved him off from the Knaresborough railway station on the first leg of his journey. I was so thankful that he was going there, and in my mind's eye, I could visualise the relief in the hospital and the excitement of the girls! Three weeks after Keith arrived, I received a desperate phone-call from BCMS. Keith had had an accident with the hospital Land Rover and had suffered a serious head injury.

He was travelling with a dresser called Francis; I knew him well. I knew the road well too, and late one night, they were travelling back from business in Kampala over very uneven roads. The narrow road took a sharp bend and his headlights suddenly lit up a broken-down truck – but it was too late to brake and he hit it head on. Keith immediately said, "We must pray;" climbed out of the crashed vehicle and both of them knelt by the side of the road. He prayed aloud for a few moments, then collapsed and never regained consciousness. The dressers managed to get Keith to Peter Cox's hospital, just over the Kenyan border, but he died a few days later.

How could we possibly get an answer to the question that we were all asking: "Why?" Perhaps the fault lay with the truck-driver who had left no warning branches laid along the road (he should have done)... perhaps night driving was not a good idea... and... but... what if God knew something unbearable which might have happened in the future? The Knaresborough Church and especially the young people were stunned and questioning, "Why God, why?" I remember that I myself descended into a deep gloom.

Andy and Bob invited all the young people to Four Quarters for a long evening session. The young people remembered Keith as the crazy choirmaster of their Youth Choir who sometimes conducted standing on his head! There was a lot of bewilderment and heart-searching as they questioned why God had allowed Keith to die. For some, that evening became a spiritual turning point. Remarkably it did not lead them to reject God but instead to turn to God, trusting Him with their own lives and future. One of them set his sights that evening on becoming a doctor.

Meanwhile, sad letters began arriving from people in Amudat. Some were from the girls in the hostel and Mary who looked after them. Justus, the lab assistant, sent news of the hospital and told me he was still running the Explorers Club on Sunday afternoons; that was encouraging. John Magal, who had been a dresser, wrote that he was now a Church Army Captain and was helping Rev. Daudi, the pastor/shopkeeper, at the church. Lomuria, that first little boy who had 'adopted' me, struggled to write to tell me how much he was missing me and that he had grown out of his shoes.

I longed with all my heart to go back to Amudat, but that part of my life was behind me. I could just grieve. I had no say in it any more. People continued asking me, "What will you do next, Ruth?" The whole wide world seemed open to me again, but with a difference – I was now 36 years old, I knew some (bad) Swahili and had ten years experience in East Africa. In the end, BCMS suggested the hospital which Lillian Singleton had just left - in another remote spot but in Tanzania, near the Rwanda/Burundi border. As nothing else appeared on the horizon, I accepted that this was what God wanted me to do.

A few months before I left, BCMS asked me to write my experiences for a book. I had the time, so I tap-tapped away on a borrowed typewriter for hours and days, recording all my memories. Someone at BCMS helped to make it readable. Then I forgot about it as I set my sights, not very enthusiastically, on preparing to go to Tanzania.

Four Quarters had enough paying guests, all Christians, to make it workable. Debi and all the others who lived there over the next few years - Alison, Peter, Jonathan, Brian, Hazel and Christine to name but some - welcomed young people and their own friends, and even older lonely folk, at hours convenient and sometimes very inconvenient. They became listening ears for youngsters and a bolt-hole for tired Christians - just what the four of us had hoped for. Even my sister Julia and her husband found a temporary home there when they moved to the UK with their toddler, Deborah-Ann. Four Quarters gave us no worries.

But now Keith was with the Lord in heaven, Andy was heading for the Sudan with CMS, Bob was getting married, and... me? I was not excited about going to Tanzania! I was only interested in Amudat, but I kept my feelings to myself. The Knaresborough folk gave me a wonderful send-off with a barn dance at Oakwood, the Webster's farm, and on my 37th birthday, 1976, this reluctant missionary flew from Heathrow Airport to Tanzania.

"Sister Ruth"

The jumbo jet from Heathrow took me to Nairobi in Kenya and from there an MAF six-seater flew me on to Tanzania. First we touched down at Mwanza, a large town on Lake Victoria, and then headed west towards Murgwanza Hospital, pronounced 'Mu-ru-gwanza'. I watched the terrain beneath me become hillier and greener. Dotted everywhere I could see shambas (small farms) surrounding the rectangular iron roofs of homes of the many peasant farmers.

Then the MAF pilot told us he'd never flown that hop before and had lost his way! He kept consulting a map strapped on his thigh and calling on his radio for directions. Fortunately there was another plane within radio calling distance and they told him that he had over-flown Murgwanza and was now over Rwanda. He was directed to a tarred, snaking road, and the pilot banked and followed the road back over the border into Tanzania. Very soon we spotted Murgwanza Hospital beneath us. The pilot buzzed it to announce our arrival, and soon we touched down on a very bumpy 'airfield'. I hopped out and stood in the shade of a tree as the pilot lifted off again, tipping his wing in farewell.

I was left standing in lush country, with banana trees waving their huge broad leaves in welcome. After about an hour, the hospital Land Rover burst through the banana trees, and I climbed in, soon understanding why the four-by-four had taken so long to reach me. We twisted and turned, bumped over ruts and slipped in the mud until we revved up a steep hill, and there at last was Murgwanza.

We were on a ridge six thousand feet above sea level where missionaries in the 1930's had started medical work. I sniffed the sharp, cool air. Three smiling Australians stepped forward to shake hands with me: Ross the pharmacist; Margaret his wife; and Beverley, the other Grade A nurse. She surprised me with the news that I was the new Matron! Doctor Arthur Adeney and his wife Jan were away in Kenya, taking their seven-year-old son to boarding school.

Beverley took me along a muddy track - past a church, some houses and a football pitch - to where I was to live. We each had half of an old mission house with thick walls of mud brick. Those long-ago missionaries certainly knew how to choose a good view; it looked over the edge of the steep ridge to the valley far below, and in the far distance I could see Rwanda, beyond the Kagera River, the Tanzanian border. Around the houses eucalyptus trees, planted by those first missionaries forty years ago, gave off their fragrance.

I was keen to see the hospital. It couldn't have been more different from Amudat - not a 'bush hospital' but one recognised by the government as the 'Designated District Hospital' with regulations and standards. There were at least ten trained Tanzanian nurses and many assistant nurses, but Beverly and I were the only Grade A nurses.

She took me around the two-storey hospital. We peered around the door of the Labour Ward; there a trained nurse was calmly delivering a baby with its usual indignant cry. The Prem Room next door had six tiny premature ones being cared for in a room warmed and humidified by a steam kettle bubbling on a primus stove. They looked cute in miniature bootees, bonnets and mitts.

Next we went upstairs via a semicircular ramp, built to wheel patients up to the Surgical Wards and Theatre. In the Theatre, I said hello to a Staff Nurse setting up for an operation. Then Beverly took me into the Matron's office and shouted with laughter as she gleefully handed over the duty timetables. I wondered why! Back downstairs we passed through the "Out Patients Department" and "Ante Natal Clinic". The doctor and a medical assistant, Mr Samugabo, both had queues of patients; it was busy, but not chaotic like Amudat.

The two Children's Wards were separated from the other departments by a covered pathway. They were crowded and noisy and included a special 'unit' for malnourished children. Mrs Nzutu, an older assistant nurse, spent her time convincing the mothers that their children had no actual illness but were suffering from Kwashiorkor – a protein deficiency. I recognised the tell-tale signs: pot-bellies; pale, dry, flaky skin; reddish hair; skinny legs; and grizzling. Each mother had to cook her own child's food in a separate mud-walled kitchen, just like the kitchen she was used to at home. Then she would watch the improvement in her child without injections and pills. Mrs Nzutu told me that at home the whole family ate out of one huge platter and the little ones naturally chose the softer, easy-to-chew food, like the cooked plantains (a type of non-sweet banana which was the staple diet). As a result they missed out on the chewy beans or meat with the protein and vitamins. So she taught the mothers to give their toddlers their own dish of food and to mash up the tough bits!

My tour ended at the hospital office. Beverley introduced me to Lazaro, the hospital administrator; then Zephania, the foreman; George, the driver; Geoffrey, the carpenter; and a whole array of staff who took my breath away when I compared it to Amudat – a pharmacist; laundry workers; night guards; and many others; even a tailor!

I soon discovered that one of my jobs was teaching the assistant nurses, including hopeful new girls. Beverly showed me a file with a thick pile of application letters from girls who were coming to the end of their primary schooling. I had to call them all in and give them a month's crash course in basic hygiene, making beds etc; then set them an exam and choose the most promising.

In spite of it being a larger, more advanced hospital, I didn't settle easily in Murgwanza. I missed the Amudat life - wild, dry, hot and unique - and I missed my Amudat friends and the boys and girls. I knew that it was unwise to compare the two places, but I couldn't help myself!

Something else was different here as well. I had never before felt a barrier between me and the people I worked with. Arthur and Jan Adeney explained that it was all to do with their struggle for Independence. Tanzania had become independent fifteen years earlier in 1961, with Julius Nyerere as its first President. In every school timetable, an important subject was Siasa - Politics. All the children were taught about each stage in the Tanzanian Independence struggle, which showed up the British in a poor light. The fact that independence came peacefully was attributed to the heroic efforts of Julius Nyerere. Expats were living reminders of their hard-won independence. I quickly learnt a new Swahili word: 'Ukoloni' - colonialism. Some of the staff were very sensitive to any hints of ukoloni. One of the staff shouted after me, "M'koloni!" (colonialist) when I had asked her to change her duty because someone was ill. Had I been wrong to ask her? Had I asked in a bossy manner? Possibly.

Jan and Arthur explained that Nyerere had from the start aimed to put his Socialist ideology into practice. Everyone was equal. 'Ndugu' (comrade) was a title you could call anyone from peasant farmer to the President himself, although he was more often referred to respectfully as Mwalimu Julius Nyerere, meaning 'Teacher' (which had been his profession). Influenced by the Chinese, he had introduced Ujamaa, a policy of 'villagisation', and tried to get Tanzanian peasants farmers to move into communes - at first voluntarily, then by legislation. But the policy was not a success and had been abandoned by the time I arrived in 1976.

The Chinese had just finished building the Tazara Railway, linking Zambia with Tanzania. At first I saw Chinese tinned food in shops, such as tins of duck in orange sauce! But soon after I arrived, the Chinese left and shortages got worse. Diesel became so scarce that the hospital was often without electricity and water. Paraffin was essential to run the pharmacy fridge where the precious store of vaccinations was kept, so the pharmacist anxiously eked out his supply of paraffin, trying to keep them at the right temperature.

We too had to be careful with our paraffin for lamps and sometimes had to abandon our paraffin fridge altogether. It became impossible to buy batteries, sugar, salt, rice, soap and even flour to make bread. Like everyone at the hospital, I had to join the Hospital Co-operative Shop - and get a number - to be eligible for a share of whatever goods came in. It was divided out equally between all the members. On the notice board outside the Administrator's offices, Lazaro would put up a notice saying, "Shop - open at 4 pm for sugar." We would queue up with a bag to get our allocation. Whatever it was, we would buy it: sugar, rice, salt, cooking oil or even a piece of cloth!

One policy which didn't fail, though, was that of making the national language Swahili. All primary schooling was in Swahili, and this helped to unify the nation with its many tribal languages. Only a few older people couldn't speak Swahili. People were proud of their national language and spoke it beautifully, and I winced at the way I unintentionally mutilated the language; my Ugandan Swahili seriously needed brushing up! The Staff Nurses had passed their nursing exams in English so spoke good English, but they all preferred Swahili.

One jolly nationwide custom that Mwalimu Nyerere introduced was the 'Mwenge'. Every year, a flaming torch was sent throughout Tanzania, following various routes. It was transported by Land Rover though village after village and town after town and handed from one person to another with lots of laughter and ululating. I knew a Roman Catholic nun who was once handed the torch to run a few metres along the road and she had been thrilled.

As Matron, besides juggling the nurse's rosters I had to oversee admissions, deal with crises, and supervise the staff – and some of this made me unpopular. I felt that the colour of my skin was seen before the sense of what I said - it was my turn to experience a bit of discrimination! I made more blunders at Murgwanza than I did at any other place.

The thing I dreaded most was the Workers' Meeting, based on the Chinese model. I used to feel sick the whole day before! The Tanzanian staff looked forward to it eagerly because this was their chance to air their grievances. There was lots of raucous laughter and shouting about the rich and shouting others down! Dr Arthur Adeney coped with it much better than I did. His parents had been missionaries in Rwanda and Burundi and he had been born and brought up there, so he could speak their tribal language almost before he could speak English. In his quiet way, he seemed to have a gift of getting through to the staff. He quoted their proverbs and made them laugh, and more often than not, the ill-feeling at the meeting just dissolved. Some of the 'stirrers' went away disgruntled, complaining that he was too 'smooth tongued'. I went home for some soothing music and a cup of tea!

Going Bananas

It was all a far cry from Amudat! On one of my days off, I wandered over to the edge of the ridge and sat hidden, with my back leaning against a rock. I felt very sorry for myself.

My eyes rested on the lovely view in the river valley. Far below I could see small homes surrounded by the bright green patches of banana trees. I saw people busy hoeing, herding and collecting water. The smoke of fires drifted upwards and evaporated into the air. An occasional voice reached my ears. I soaked in the peace. In the distance were the many hills of Rwanda, grey and misty, and in-between snaked the Kagera River, outlined by shades of green, becoming most vivid at the river's edge. This was our border with Rwanda. By screwing up my eyes, I could just make out the conical volcanic mountains on Rwanda's far border with the Congo, where the mountain gorillas lived. It was all so beautiful and yet I still felt sorry for myself. In Amudat I had been everybody's 'Little Sister'; here I was just 'Mkoloni'. I silently cried, "Lord, if I must live here, please enable me to enjoy it!"

Not long afterwards, there was a Convention at the Murgwanza Church – a week-long series of meetings with long, inspiring sermons. I sat on the left hand side of the church, squashed among the women and girls. The men sat on the right-hand side, less squashed! I read the Bible verse chosen for the week. It was printed on cardboard and strung across the front of the church: "TAZAMA, NINAFANYA JAMBO JIPYA". My Swahili was not yet up to it, so I looked in my English Bible and read, "See, I am doing a new thing." I felt that God was speaking to me personally, and I prayed, "Please send me this 'new thing' quickly!"

Knowing how hard I was finding things, Jan and Arthur Adeney reassured me.

"When you get to know some of the Christians, you'll realise that there are some lovely friendly people here."

Very soon after this I received my first invitation to a Tanzanian home. I met Martha at the weekly church Fellowship and found that Bartimeu, a handyman at the hospital, was her husband. Martha arranged for her husband to collect me after work one day and to visit them. So he led me through rustling banana plantations to their small home, which was surrounded by yet more rustling bananas. Martha prepared a meal from their own home-grown produce - plantains (or green bananas) with mushy yellow peas - delicious!

Martha told me about different kinds of bananas, all with different purposes. Plantains are a variety of big bananas that are not left to go yellow but peeled while green and hard; then cooked and mashed to make a staple dish, tasting like mashed potato. Another variety made banana juice - I would taste this at weddings - also delicious! Yet another variety was used for making pombe (beer). I was told that this was potent stuff. Anglican Christians took a firm stand against beer-drinking. Pombe usually led to drunkenness which led in turn to fighting, unwanted pregnancies and messed up marriages. On the way home it started to rain; Bartimeu darted into the banana trees and broke off a huge banana leaf.

"Use that as an umbrella!"

As the weeks passed, more people invited me to their homes and they in turn came to visit me. Outside my door I would hear "Hodi", which was how they 'knocked' on the door. The reply is "Karibu", meaning 'come in'. I remember one friendly Christian woman arriving with the usual call of "Hodi!" I went to the door and saw Etheri with a basket on her head, and I invited her in.

"Karibu, karibu!"

She just stood motionless in my doorway, frowning.

Again I said, "Karibu, karibu."

Looking exasperated, she complained, "How many times do I have to give you missionaries a seminar on what to do when someone visits you?"

I looked blank.

She instructed, "You must take whatever I have on my head because it's a gift for you! If you don't take it, it's like saying you don't want it. It's very rude!"

Quickly I lifted up my hands as she lowered the basket. I saw a plastic bag of yellow peas, some peanuts in their shells and several hands of sweet bananas.

In those days of shortages, sweet bananas were a real lifesaver - such a versatile food. At breakfast, we sliced them up; sprinkled with milk and sugar, we called them 'cereal'. At elevenses we called them 'biscuits' and ate them with our coffee, sometimes dunking one end of the banana into a dish of roasted peanuts. In the evening we might fry them, squeeze in orange juice, and call them 'dessert'!

On Saturdays, my day off, I was often taken to the market with some of the off-duty nurses - down the ridge from the Hospital, through shady forests of banana trees, to our nearest small town, Ngara. It consisted of a number of shops, the bus stand and the post office where the Murgwanza Hospital Post Bag was delivered by bus from Mwanza. The marketplace was simply a large piece of bare ground where local people brought fruit and veg to sell. They spread out long banana leaves and built little piles of bananas, oranges and tomatoes, to sell them by the heap. Bargaining was the custom and I quickly picked up that art. I filled my rucksack and puffed the mile back up the hill. The girls all carried their heavy purchases gracefully on their heads in a basket; it looked so easy but I never learnt to do it.

The Adeneys were right; my happiest times at Murgwanza were with the Christians and visiting the churches in the surrounding villages. Whenever I went to Jan and Arthur's, I would meet visiting Tanzanian pastors and evangelists and they often invited me to their churches. These were scattered over large areas - one parish consisted of fifteen churches, dotted over ridges and valleys. I began to go with a group of young people or a church youth choir to these outlying churches. Some churches were near, no more than five miles, so we set off early on Sunday morning. Others were further afield so I borrowed a vehicle to get us there, possibly sleeping overnight. I enjoyed these breaks away from the Hospital.

On one occasion I took a group of young assistant nurses with me in the hospital Land Rover. After church and lunch, we were on our way home and the girls were singing enthusiastically, when suddenly the Land Rover's engine died. The petrol gauge showed empty. The girls were horrified; we were a long, long way from home and some of us were on duty next morning. Trying to be a good example, I suggested we pray, and they all thought that was a good idea. We stood in a huddle and prayed aloud. Into my mind trickled a very faint memory and I thought, "Didn't Arthur tell me that the Land Rover has two tanks?" I extricated myself from the huddle and half-heartedly searched under the driver's seat. I noticed an insignificant looking switch and flipped it down. Then I tried the engine and it sprung into life! They stared at me in awe. Then they all piled in and we drove off, singing about the miracle.

The Fire, it is lit today!
The Fire, it is the work of Jesus!
The Fire, it is lit today. Sing, Alleluia! The Fire burns!

I began to get more and more invitations to churches, not only with the young people but also on my own, in which I was invited to preach. I enjoyed this, in spite of nights on hard floors and rats pattering by. But I kept looking out for that 'new thing' God had promised me, which seemed to be such a long time coming.

One hot Saturday afternoon, I was trudging on my own the ten miles to speak at a church next day. Suddenly I recognised Andrew, a young evangelist, riding towards me on a dilapidated bike.

"Pastor has sent me to meet you and give you a lift," he panted.

Delighted, I bounced up and sat side saddle on the luggage rack (as ladies did) with my kanga, a brightly coloured traditional cloth, wrapped over my skirt for modesty. Andrew bumped along, puffing furiously up the hills and it certainly shortened the journey.

On another occasion, I went to a church with one of my colleagues, Judy. For our overnight stay we were given a single, narrow, home-made bed to sleep on; instead of a mattress the rough, wooden frame was covered with cowhide. Even with sleeping bags it was very hard and we had to turn over in unison all night.

Once I went on a three day conference where I shared a small mud-walled room with Jean, the Mothers' Union Worker. A kind lady thoughtfully brought us one basin of hot water to have a total body wash. We stood there looking at each other, embarrassed.

The lady said, "You are both unmarried young women; you've nothing to be embarrassed about! Wash!"

So we washed - after a fashion.

Staying overnight with the pastors and their families, I learnt more about their lives, which to me seemed tough. Like most people, the pastors were also hard-working, small farmers. The land was very fertile. There were three harvests per year: the first, during the long rains; the next, during the short rains; and the third, by deliberately flooding their fields. This meant they could grow all their own food, but they still needed money for school uniforms, tea, sugar, paraffin, roofing and furniture. So they had to sell some of their produce and even grow cash crops; coffee fetched good prices but it took a lot of 'tender loving care' to get good coffee beans.

My friends patiently explained to me that Tanzania followed a Socialist philosophy which meant that no one actually owned land. If you cultivated a patch of ground, no one could take it from you because the crop belonged to you, so you had secured that piece of land; neglect it and you might find someone else busy there with a hoe! So if you planted a coffee orchard, you could secure the land to pass on to the next generation.

Our friends were extremely generous and we missionaries were blessed with an abundance of gifts, though never coffee. Sometimes after a difficult day at the hospital, when I was feeling sorry for myself, I would hear "hodi" at my door, and I would find that someone with a gift balanced on her head was waiting for my "karibu". Sometimes it was a child with a heavy, two-foot-long stick of bananas on her head, cushioned with a coiled up cloth pad.

"Mama sent you these, Sister!"

That helped a lot to cope with the difficult times.

Because of the three harvests a year, we had three Harvest Thanksgivings! More than once, I saw a man stagger into church with a huge stick of bananas and lay it in front of the communion table. Behind him came his wife carrying dried kidney beans, wrapped up in a kanga, and behind her, their children with more gifts – perhaps a cabbage or a clucking hen. There were often eggs in the offering plate.

An amazing number of the churches dotting the valleys and ridges had their beginnings in the 1930's when the East African Revival spread to Tanzania from Burundi and Rwanda. At huge meetings, crowds of people were converted and built large burnt-brick churches. Those first converts had prospered partly because they gave up drink (and therefore drunkenness) and the men stuck to one wife only. Family life flourished and money went further. They were interested in new ideas for growing crops, so with more money, they were able to help their children get a good education. When I arrived in Tanzania, there were many Christian families belonging to well-established churches.

I also came across many 'baby' churches. They sprang up when a young man or woman was dramatically converted but found no church near their home. The pastor of the whole Parish would encourage them to start one. I was amazed at their confidence, holding services under trees or squashed into windowless classrooms. As the congregation grew, they got together to build a special hut, with mud walls and a thatched roof, and with dried, sweet-smelling grass to sit on. The young leaders (called Evangelists or Church Teachers) led services, Sunday Schools, youth groups, choirs and much more. If they showed promise and dedication, the pastor sent them to the Diocesan Bible School in Mwanza.

One of the highlights for these Christian young people was a Kesha (Watch Night Service). Every month, young people from the many village churches converged at one of the big churches for the whole night! Each group came prepared with a new song. When the Kesha was held at Murgwanza, I would hear all the different choirs arriving, singing their special songs. At intervals throughout the night, an elder or pastor taught from the Bible, challenging them about their Christian lives. There was lots of singing, usually with percussion instruments: drums, guitars, rattles and even a ridged coke bottle rubbed with a key. On into the night, some of the young people told their own stories: their struggles to live a Christ-like life and how they had failed, repented and the Lord Jesus had forgiven them. Sometimes one of them suddenly 'saw the light' and was dramatically 'saved'. Everyone leapt up in excitement, and some woke up and danced, clapped and praised God.   Some of our assistant nurses regularly attended the Murgwanza Kesha and still managed to come to work next morning. Wide-eyed but yawning, they told me what a wonderful time they'd had.

"Sister, you should have been there; Paulo was saved!"

Is This the New Thing?

On 16th February, 1977, I woke up to shocking news. My dear friend Janani Luwuum, the archbishop of Uganda, had been killed in a car accident. We all guessed at once that he had been murdered, and soon this was confirmed on the BBC Overseas Service. I thought back to how he had been such a comfort to us when I was arrested and how he had gone to see Idi Amin. When peoples' loved ones disappeared they had run to him for help, and Janani Luwuum had been fearless in confronting Amin about atrocities which he and his henchmen were committing. Finally, Amin tired of him and summoned him to a meeting. The archbishop knew what was coming but went to the meeting regardless – a modern Ugandan martyr.

I had written a little book about how Archbishop Luwuum had rescued me from prison; it was published a few months later under the title 'Amudat Sister', and being so topical it sold well. Idi Amin continued to make headline news. The book had an unexpected side effect. BCMS began to think that I might have a hidden talent as a writer! The author Rhena Taylor suggested I attend her Christian Communications Course at Daystar College in Nairobi. My heart beat quicker and I asked myself, "Could this be the 'new thing' which God promised me?"

I left by bus, bumping all night the 270 miles to Mwanza, where I caught an MAF plane to Nairobi. It was wonderful not to have the responsibility of the hospital! After so many years, becoming a student again was great fun. We studied every kind of communication you can imagine: African Christian music, radio talks, graphic design, magazine profiles, newspaper reporting, and much more – all in four months! It was stimulating to be in a class with so many nationalities – pastors and teachers from Kenya, Rwanda, Tanzania and Zambia, a nun from Sudan, 'Youth for Christ' workers from Nigeria and Ghana, and even students from Japan and Germany.

Did you know we all wear cultural spectacles? It was brought home to us all in the classroom when an American tutor asked us, "What do you do in your culture to show a girl you're interested in her?"

The Zambian volunteered, "I'd ask her for her photo."

A Nigerian said, "I'd go and talk to her parents."

The German girl piped up, "Hopefully he'd ask me out for a coffee."

Then one of us asked the American tutor, "What would they do in America?"

She drawled, "Well, he might send her flowers."

The class erupted into laughter, shouting incredulously, "Leaves! Give her leaves?"

In the middle of my Communications Course we had heard that Idi Amin had ordered bombing in Tanzania, near the Uganda border. This had enraged the Tanzanians and they had sent their troops to the border; now a war raged.

I finished the course with a few American grades up my sleeve, many new friends and some stimulating new ideas sprouting in my head. But while I was still in Kenya, and before going back to Tanzania, there was something I simply had to do without going into Uganda. I wanted to get near as possible to Amudat. This was my dream! So I squeezed into an already overflowing Rift Valley Peugeot taxi. To loud African music, I hurtled at hair-raising speeds down the Rift Valley and onwards to Kitale (the Kenyan town nearest to Amudat). There I caught a bus.

I sat in the noisy bus as it slowly wound its way down the steep escarpment in low gear. It stopped in the evening at Kacheliba - still in Kenya but only thirty miles short of Amudat. As I stepped off the bus, I felt the warm air on my bare arms. I breathed it in and all the memories flooded back. Yes... of course... that's what the evening air used to feel like... not burningly hot... just comfortably warm. I had forgotten, in those four years, the warm, dry smell... the thorny, leafless trees in the moonlight, silhouetted like cardboard cut-outs... and the sandy road, a white ribbon between the trees with houses crouched low on either side.

Samwel, one of my old Amudat friends and now a Chief, materialised out of the darkness and led me to his house. Inside, there was Lokeno, reading his Bible - the very same ex-schoolboy whom the doctor diagnosed with a thyroid deficiency. He was now an evangelist! He looked up with his typical slow smile. Both Samwel and Lokeno had been among those I had sipped tea with in the old days, learning so much about their ways.

Samwel said, "I found him a job here in Kenya, but he refused it because he won't leave the people in Amudat."

The door burst open. Six girls rushed in.

"Is it you, Sister; is it really you?"

A large teenager flung herself upon me and pressed her cheek to mine.

"Yes, it's me," I replied, tears streaming down my cheeks. "But who are you? It's not Leah, is it?"

But it *was* Leah!

Then followed, "Do you remember who this is? What about this one? Don't you remember Agnes?"

I strained in the light of a small hurricane lamp to recognise them all. How they had grown! Hugs and tears continued all round with the once little girls from our hostel. Then I noticed one girl standing behind the others, trying to hide her very pregnant figure under a kanga. They laughingly dragged Mary into our joint embrace.

"You speak such good English, Leah" I exclaimed.

"Yes, Sister, I go to Alliance Girls' High School in Kenya. I'm the first Amudat girl to go there."

"Do you like it?"

"No, Sister, I don't like it because it is so far from home, and my mother doesn't know how to write so she can't send me letters. But God is helping me to stay there."

Samwel's wife, Julia, who had also been at school in Amudat, gave me a mug of tea. Another memory flooded back. The tea was made of pure milk, without water; I had forgotten the peculiar tang with its hint of charcoal. Over tea, we talked into the night, catching up on four years' news.

"You wouldn't like to see Amudat Hospital now," they told me. "It's just a shell. The doors and windows have been stolen. Musa stayed to look after it."

They told me that some deserting Ugandan soldiers had sold their Kalashnikovs to the Pokot men, who went on a drunken rampage. They raided the Amudat shops, broke down the hospital doors and ripped the Land Rover tyres. Only the church was left untouched. Everyone fled – police, shopkeepers, teachers and hospital staff. The church pastor/shopkeeper, Rev. Daudi, had fought with a Pokot warrior in his shop till a gourd of milk fell off a hook and burst on the floor with a sound like a gunshot. The warrior ran away and Daudi fled with his family over the border.

More young men who had also been schoolboys in Amudat slipped in to join us. I finally asked the question that had worried me ever since I heard that Liza Cox had distributed my little book 'Amudat Sister' to everyone.

"Did the book I wrote upset you or annoy you? Was any of it untrue?"

"No, no," Samwel replied, "it was all true. But it made us so sad, because it reminded us of the good things that were spoilt because of Amin."

Daniel reminisced, "It was just like you said; we often sat at night, and talked and talked. Those were good days."

Porit turned to me in the dim light.

"Sister, do you remember the song we sang at hospital prayers on the morning you were taken?"

I shook my head.

He smiled. "After you had gone, it comforted us."

He started to sing, and everyone quietly joined in.

I know who holds the future and He'll guide me with His hand,
With God things don't just happen, everything by God is planned.
So as I face tomorrow with its problems large and small,
I'll trust the God of miracles, give to Him my all.

Late in the night, after prayers, Julia gave me a safari bed to sleep on with cool, clean sheets. Before falling asleep, I looked around the darkened room and counted ten mounds on the floor, all sleeping girls. In the next room there were about the same number of mounds, all sleeping boys. Three were blind boys on their way back to boarding school. All of them were being helped by Samwel, now the respected Christian chief of Kacheliba. As I dozed I recalled what one girl had told me: "I began to follow Jesus when I saw you being taken away!" I started to cry.

When I awoke early next morning, Samwel had already taken the blind boys to catch their bus. Reluctantly, I had to catch mine, back up the escarpment to Kitale. A forgotten memory suddenly flashed into my mind. Four years ago I had taken a painting to be framed in Kitale. It had been painted by an artistic teacher called Jacob, and I had forgotten all about it for the four years.

On a whim, I made my way to the Asian shop where I had left it and asked, without any real hope, "You don't know what happened to that picture I brought here years ago, do you?"

The man turned away and picked something up.

"Do you mean this one?"

He held it up above the counter - it was the very one!

A few days later I flew back to Tanzania with my painting. Murgwanza was still not my favourite place, in spite of the Christian fellowship I had started to enjoy. But I tried to settle down to being Matron again.

During my four months' absence, the war with Uganda had caused problems for the hospital. Some of the trained nurses had been drafted into the army, so we were short-staffed and once more I had to perspire over rosters. There was also a new compulsory activity for all able-bodied Tanzanians, called 'Mchaka-mchaka.' Its purpose was to toughen everyone up, just in case the Uganda War spread. I had to roster staff so that they could report to the Comrade Leader in the early mornings. Still snuggled up in bed, I listened to them singing political songs as they ran up and down the hills and round and round the football pitch. No one was exempt. I felt sorry for the nurses when they came on duty, exhausted after all the up-hill running; but not one of them ever complained.

The time for my UK leave was drawing near. Beverley became Matron and I was allowed to do something new - helping the pastors in the rural churches. Sometimes the Rural Dean took me on the back of his motorbike over precarious roads visiting remote churches. Canon Kuboko was elderly and had high blood pressure, so it helped if I preached and he gave Holy Communion and saw to the many pastoral problems. I wondered if this was the 'new thing' God had promised me... but I was wrong!

Mwanza, Tanzania 1980 – 1990

"Mama Kaseti"

The time for my UK leave finally arrived, and I eagerly made my way to 'Four Quarters' in Knaresborough. Missionaries were always reminded that coming to England was not a holiday but 'Home Assignment'! The Mission sent Anne Wright to debrief me - the very same one who had been such a 'rock' during my imprisonment in Uganda, now working as Northern Rep for BCMS.

She handed me my programme:

- a few weeks with my family in South Africa;
- a week camping at Keswick Convention;
- opening a Garden Party in Lancaster;
- medical check-ups in London;
- attending the BCMS Committee (explain what I'd been doing and answer questions);
- official visits to my ten supporting parishes, and others.

I wailed to Anne, "But I didn't do well in Murgwanza. It wasn't like Amudat - I don't have such good stories."

Anne smiled sympathetically but told me I had no choice – the churches were all expecting me. Nonetheless, I began to enjoy meeting all the kindly friends I'd made over the years. I set out at Ditton in Kent and then went to Wandsworth in London. From there I travelled north to Nottingham and Stapleford where there were more happy reunions, then on further north to Normanton, near Leeds - more hugs and smiles. I looked forward to going to Blackpool over the Pennines to see the old church where it all began with my parents becoming Christians and staying with my godmother. Then over to the east to Brough, near Hull, and finally, to a cluster of village churches around Great Smeaton, in North Yorkshire. Sometimes, when I woke up in the morning, I asked myself, "Which town am I in?" Sometimes, I even wondered, "Which *country* am I in?"

Some of the vicars worked me hard - up to five sermons a Sunday; that was in North Yorkshire, trying to get around all five village churches. The visit I remember most vividly was at Stapleford in Nottingham. There were two churches and I had to go to both. St Helen's started at 10.30 am and the service at St Andrews at 10.45. They wanted me to speak at both, so after speaking early on in the service at St Helen's, I was rushed to St Andrews in the middle of the service. Walking breathless down the aisle at St Andrews, I was given little waves and grins of welcome; but apart from the family where I'd slept the night, the faces were just a blur. I stepped up into the pulpit and felt I ought to begin with an apology.

"I'm so sorry I didn't recognise some of you when I came in just now, but I see so many people, I only remember those I sleep with."

There was a titter around the congregation. I turned red.

While in UK, I was reunited with my old friends the Coxes from Amudat days! They had finally returned to the UK after twenty-one years. Peter was Course Director for overseas medical students at Leeds University. He amazed me with the following recollection.

"One day, Ruth, just after you were deported from Uganda, I was on safari and stuck on the far side of the flooded river at Amudat. As we all sat around a campfire an old Pokot man, also stranded, entertained me with a song: 'Chepocoggis, Amin sent Chepocoggis to her own country. Chepocoggis wasn't very tall.'"

Peter turned to me.

"Chepocoggis, you are now remembered in the traditional songs of the Pokot tribe!"

Home Assignment usually lasted six months, approximately two months for every year away. Early 1980, I farewelled Four Quarters, Knaresborough and BCMS and flew back to Tanzania, as usual via Kenya, and then south by MAF plane. It touched down at the small airport in Mwanza (not to be confused with Murgwanza), 270 miles west, where the hospital is. Ross Hall met me, Diocesan Administrator and Australia CMS missionary.

He announced in his Australian drawl, "Now that you're so well trained in communications, the bishop wants you to start a cassette ministry here in Mwanza."

I thought to myself, "Little do they know it but I didn't learn anything about that!" Out loud I said, "I haven't a clue what to do."

"No worries; we'll send you to see how the Australian 'mishoes' started it up in Dodoma. Go on to Murgwanza now and get packing!"

I waved goodbye.

"Where will I live?" I shouted to Ross.

"No worries; we'll see you right, mate," he replied airily.

The plane set off over Lake Victoria. Suddenly I gasped. Was I seeing things? I saw a rainbow forming a complete circle in the air! The pilot said that they called it 'The Glory', and he banked the plane for my eyes to take it in. It was like a sign from God; this was the 'new thing'!

At Murgwanza, I packed my stuff and waited for a bus - unpredictable in those days, as fuel was still scarce and spare parts in short supply. Eventually Lazaro the Hospital Administrator brought the news: a bus had arrived from Mwanza and would turn around in the morning. So early next day, I piled all my things on the roof rack of a battered-looking bus - three cardboard boxes and a suitcase – and I settled down for the 270 miles of unmade roads to Mwanza.

It was a slow journey. The bus kept stopping to pile in more passengers, who always argued about the fare. The sun went down and I dozed in spite of the bumpy road. Three times that night we were stopped at road blocks. Police stuck their heads around the door of the bus.

"Passengers, get out!" they barked and we sleepily lined up outside. Then they shouted, "Line up all your bags here... yes, even the ones on top of the bus!"

We all meekly obeyed, without argument. I climbed up the iron ladder on the side of the bus and some passengers helped me lower my four loads to the ground. After a cursory glance, the police told us to put everything back again! No one had any idea what they were looking for.

At 3 am, after only one puncture, we arrived within sight of

Mwanza. A few lights from the town twinkled across the final stretch of water, Mwanza Gulf (an inlet of Lake Victoria), but we were far too late for the last ferry. Some of the passengers smoked, talked, joked and laughed loudly while the rest dozed or snored. All the windows were closed against mosquitoes so it became hot and stuffy. I couldn't bear it any longer and went outside, climbed the ladder onto the roof and dozed amongst the luggage, alongside long sticks of bananas and whining mosquitoes, with a kanga over my head.

Early the next morning, I was sipping sweet milky tea at a roadside stall when the ferry chugged up to the shingle. The ramp was lowered, the bus bounced on and we followed wearily on board. In less than an hour it deposited us on the edge of Mwanza Town, the Regional Capital - my new home for the next ten years.

People were busily going about their work. Women near the ferry tended small charcoal stoves, tempting hungry travellers with mugs of sweet tea and maandazi (doughnuts). Further along the shore, hungry birds shrieked and squabbled over dead fish heads, while fishermen sold their night's catch. Muscular young men then pushed the fish to market. I saw some carting an enormous Nile Perch – a nodding head and sightless eyes over one side of a wheelbarrow and tail shaking over the other. The huge fat fish quivered all over as it was jolted over the rough road.

"So this is the 'new thing' God promised me," I told myself.

That was in 1976; it was now 1980.

First stop was the nearby offices of the Diocese, just next door to the General Post Office. Ross Hall was in his office and he showed me where I was to live - a roomy single storey house across the road and next to the church. I didn't mind about the holes in the ceiling; at least they were stuffed with newspaper. I was pleased to be living near Lake Victoria because it is so beautiful, though I knew I would never swim there because of bilharzia, a lake parasite which needs us humans in order to burrow into our insides to lay its eggs.

Back in Ross's office, I asked a pressing question.

"How shall I run this... er... cassette ministry?"

He didn't reply, just bent his head in a drawer of his desk and rummaged around. Eventually, in triumph, he held up a screwdriver.

"There you are; start with this!"

I knocked on Bishop John's office door, still clutching my screwdriver. The Tanzanian bishop was at his desk and welcomed me warmly.

I asked him, "Where shall I set up the... er... cassette ministry?"

He replied, "Well, your house would do, wouldn't it?"

So that was decided.

It felt strange to have so many other missionaries around. Besides Ross Hall the Australian with his wife Margaret and their four children, Barbara and Jenny taught at the Bible School; Jean, the Mothers' Union worker lived with them; Geraldine was the bishop's secretary; and there were no fewer than six teachers at the English Primary School.

They all seemed so busy and over-stretched and welcomed me with (I felt) relief.

"Welcome, Ruth! You've come just when we need extra help! Will you co-ordinate the Pastors' Wives Course before you set up the cassette office?"

I couldn't refuse. But at the same time, besides that screwdriver, I gradually gathered together more equipment from Ross's overflowing office: cassettes, players and one high quality cassette recorder with microphone. I set it up in a spare room of my house, and there was my cassette office!

No sooner had the Pastors' Wives Course finished than the local churches started preparing for a national Christian Convention in the nearby football stadium, with Bishop Festo Kivengere as the main speaker. Again I found they needed spare hands and feet. Visitors would be arriving from all over Tanzania and were to be accommodated in a huge boys' boarding school. We discovered that most of the flush toilets were blocked, so some of us had to set about unblocking them. Amazingly, in spite of all the shortages in the shops, we were able to buy as many toilet brushes as we needed.

However, food was still hard to come by. I spent frustrating hours queuing up in government offices with requests for food, which

Geraldine had typed on diocesan headed notepaper with the bishop's rubber stamp. Often the person needed to put on the government rubber stamp was out and had locked the precious rubber stamp in a cupboard.

During the convention I managed to fit in my first real bit of cassette ministry work. I rushed around the stadium, setting up equipment and recording talks and songs, looking as if I knew what I was doing. I felt I was working at the forefront of modern technology. In spite of my inexperience, a useful library of sermons and Tanzanian-style singing began to be built up.

Ross told me that Gospel Recordings in Australia had invented a cassette player which worked with a handle. The player was very clever because it always went round at the correct speed, however fast or slow you wound it; but you could never stop winding it altogether, even for a moment, or it immediately stopped. It seemed ideal because batteries were still as 'scarce as hens' teeth'.

I was able to appreciate the value of a cassette ministry because I had seen in the Murgwanza area the difficulties the church leaders faced as they faithfully trudged up and down ridges and valleys to minister to remote churches and villages. But I still had little idea how to go about it.

I was able to visit two places to pick up tips: first to Dodoma, Tanzania's Capital, where a cassette ministry had been started by Australian missionaries, and then to Kasulu, in the far West of Tanzania, bordering Lake Tanganyika.

An important part of the Ministry seemed to be the Cassette Bible School (CBS). The Dodoma Cassette Ministry had pioneered this and recorded very good Christian teaching in Swahili. Ross had managed to record a very professional introduction to the courses for our Diocese. It announced in Swahili, with an appropriate 'ding-dong', "This is the Voice of Victoria Nyanza. Welcome to the Cassette Bible School. Listen to the teaching on the tape and then answer the questions in your work book."

"How can I get this started?" I asked myself. The answer lay in the Bible School five miles outside Mwanza. At that time, the principal was

93

Barbara Spring, with two teachers, Rev. Masanja Ngwesso and Jenny Shepherd. They ran three-monthly courses, and pastors from all points of the diocese sent promising young men and women evangelists to give them more training. Barbara suggested that I give weekly sessions on cassette ministry and the CBS, and she fitted it into the timetable.

Friends in England had given me a Honda 90 (called a pikipiki in Swahili), so once a week it took me the five miles to the Bible School. I threaded my way in and out of the traffic, potholes, chickens and pedestrians. Sometimes all the traffic patiently stopped while a polio victim calmly crossed the road on all fours. I remember one young lady crawling across the busy road with flip-flops on her hands and knees and balancing a pot on her head.

The students at the Nyakato Bible School became my CBS students for the term, and I led them through the first CBS course on the cassettes so that they would learn how to lead the courses and mark the workbooks. At the end of the term they were presented with a CBS Certificate.

I told them hopefully, "If you would like to lead similar courses at your own church, all you need to do is to explain to your church members and collect five shillings from each one. Bring it back to me in the cassette office here in Mwanza and I'll give you your cassettes and workbooks."

They left Bible School at the end of the term, full of enthusiasm. In my cassette office, I waited and waited for a few, at least, to come back to Mwanza for their first course. No one came. I tried to cheer myself up.

"Don't forget how huge the diocese is - as big as Wales! Where will they even find the bus-fare to get back here? Be patient!" I lectured myself.

I had almost given up hope, when one day a young man came into the office. I recognised him as one of the students, but couldn't recall his name.

"Hujambo," I greeted him in Swahili, and I added the rest of the polite greetings like, "How was your safari?"

He told me his name was Mathayo Kasagara and he had just arrived on a bus which he had boarded the night before. Then he quietly put money on the desk.

"Here are the fees for fifteen people who want to start the CBS course!"

When Mathayo had finished that course, he came back for a second course and then another... and another. I travelled to his village, a hundred miles away, to present all his students with their certificates, and I found he had even more students keen to start.

The Cassette Bible School was taking off. More church leaders began courses, and I found it harder and harder to keep the office open while visiting their churches. I asked Bishop John if there was any chance of a Tanzanian to assist me. His reaction was discouraging and he never brought up the subject again, so I gave up the idea.

One morning, early, Mathayo opened the office door.

"Are you starting another course?" I laughed.

"No, Mwalimu (teacher) Bishop sent me a message to come to Mwanza. I thought he wanted me to cut his grass, but he told me to report to you!"

Hurrah, I had an assistant!

A Team of Three

Mathayo and I spent many hours putting together CBS workbooks. This was before the days of photocopiers; so we 'cut' stencils on a typewriter, duplicated them using a moody duplicator, collated the pages, and finally stapled them into booklets. We usually ended up covered in duplicator ink.

At first we had nowhere to record our own material except outdoors, but then I read how to make an improvised studio:

- Find a huge cardboard carton of the size a fridge would be packed in.
- Line it with egg boxes.
- Cut a hole in it for the electric leads.
- And, abracadabra, there it is!

Mathayo tried sitting inside the cardboard carton with a microphone and he read a script, perspiring profusely. Our studio seemed better than nothing for recording teaching. But choirs still had to be recorded out of doors.

The only place we could find for this studio was in my guest bedroom, which was fine until I had a visitor. Our Mission's General Secretary, John Ball, came on an official visit, and he had to share the guest room with this 'studio'. Mwanza was plagued with mosquitoes and we always slept under mosquito nets, so I rigged up a temporary net for John, and I tied one corner of the net to the top of the 'studio'. It wasn't as secure as I had hoped, and in the middle of the night it collapsed on him. Poor John couldn't work out who was attacking him.

In the morning, I proudly showed John the cassette office with its pile of broken cassette players which church leaders had returned to us. Mathayo was cleaning the heads of the cassette players. He unscrewed their backs and showed John the small cockroaches running around inside - reminding us that most people lived in mud-walled houses, often sharing a room with the peanut or maize harvest. Mathayo did his best and cleaned them, and I had even less idea what to do. Then we heard the good news that CMS Australia was sending an electronic technician to work with us!

Daryl Milligan arrived with Jeni, his wife. He was a tall, quietly-spoken Australian with a bushy beard. He worked magic on all the machines and taught Mathayo some of the secrets of electronics. He picked things up quickly. The three of us began to work well together.

Mathayo gave us nicknames! Daryl Milligan was Mr Slow-w-w because of the deliberate way he went about things. I was Miss Rush-Rush, for some unknown reason. Mathayo didn't give himself a nickname, but I thought Mr Problem was a good name. Often he burst into the office saying, "Daryl, Ruth, I have a problem!" Daryl immediately downed his soldering iron, and Mathayo would tell us his problem; it was usually a theological or moral issue. With Daryl's Presbyterian upbringing, Mathayo was not allowed to get away with any woolly or unbiblical thinking, and between us we gave him a hard time - all to the good, as it turned out in later years!

We divided the work between us, and I was the one who usually went on cassette safaris. I serviced the players and exchanged cassettes as well as encouraging the students and presenting their certificates. Mostly I travelled by local buses, which were always crowded, usually late and often broke down. Occasionally, if it wasn't too far, I went by pikipiki. I became expert at squeezing the cassette equipment into the panniers and strapping a camp bed and sleeping bag onto the back.

One of those safaris, which I optimistically thought I could do by pikipiki, was by Lake Steamer to an island on Lake Victoria. I hadn't realised that the steamer would arrive in pitch darkness. When it was my turn to disembark, I started the little engine and pushed my pikipiki down the gangplank, peering into the shadows, trying to make out what was ahead. My headlight worked by a dynamo, so at such a low speed it only gave out a feeble glimmer. The captain was anxious to get away to the next island, and everyone shouted at me to hurry up.

I managed to get onto the jetty, but I couldn't see that there was a steep bank facing me which I had to drive up. The little engine petered out leaving me perched precariously on the slope, clinging to the pikipiki. From all sides came raucous laughter at the efforts of this little Mzungu woman. Eventually someone had pity on me and helped to push it up the bank onto the narrow footpath.

John, the church evangelist, met me with his bicycle and led the way along a narrow footpath which snaked between growing crops of maize and banana trees. I was relieved when I saw a dark building looming. It was the home of a church elder who showed me a room and helped me put up my safari bed. Next time I opened my eyes it was daylight.

John showed me around the island and their new church. The building had stalled at three cement blocks high, so I took a photo of him with his church elder sitting on the blocks. They explained that a big problem was getting cement to the island, and there was no money till harvest. We wandered around with a crowd of young people. One of them turned the handle of the cassette machine to play Swahili Christian songs, while his friend carried a loudspeaker linked to the machine by a cable. Everyone looked up from their hoeing to see what all the commotion was about.

I did the usual business of servicing the player and changing cassettes. Then, after a delicious lunch of freshly caught lake fish, there was a special church service in which CBS certificates were presented and I gave a talk. I spoke about the power of God's Word and I illustrated my talk with a conjuring trick I had prepared at home. I showed the word BIBLIA on a large sheet of paper, and then I tore it into small pieces as a sign that some people didn't believe the Bible or were too lazy to read it. I squashed the torn pieces up in my fist and shouted out, "The Word of the Lord endures forever!" Simultaneously I unravelled the sheet of paper with the word BIBLIA whole again! There was a near riot, and John had to jump up and explain that Mama Kaseti was not performing magic, it was only a trick!

My return journey was less tiring because the steamer left the island in daylight and a crowd of young people were there to help me on board and wave me off. Watching their cheerful faces and enthusiastic singing made everything worthwhile. It was obvious to everyone, though, that the pikipiki wasn't really adequate and we needed a suitable vehicle. After a long, long process, an organisation which helps with Christian Literature, 'Feed the Minds', gave us a grant, and Ross ordered a small, blue four-wheel-drive Suzuki from Japan. Daryl rigged up curtains in the back so I could sleep in it. He taught Mathayo to drive it, and at last we were well away.

Mathayo was my fellow driver on the first safaris in the Suzuki. We took it across the lake by ferry and then along tracks to a settlement on the lakeside. We were close to a historic monument - the steamboat in which Alexander Mackay, the great Ugandan missionary, crossed Lake Victoria en route to Uganda in 1878. (He was driven out of Uganda in 1887 and died near here, in Tanzania, in 1890.) I was immediately impressed with Mathayo's ingenuity. He quickly rigged up a loudspeaker to the car battery and played Swahili songs over the air, interspersed with Christian messages. He set out our box of books on the car bonnet, and soon passers-by were buying them, the most popular being Bibles and the Swahili translation of 'I Love Idi Amin' by Bishop Festo Kivengere. I heard people laughing incredulously, "How can anyone possibly love Idi Amin?!"

In my memory, most of my safaris seem to have merged together, but one still stands out. It was Easter weekend and I was with Pastor Abednego Masanja. His main church was on the mainland, on the west side of Lake Victoria, but he also looked after a church on Meisome Island. Our programme was to go to the island on Good Friday, and then come back to the mainland for Easter Saturday evening when I would show film strips.

The Suzuki took us to the shore of the Lake and there we waited... and waited... and waited. Eventually a large rowing boat arrived. We stacked our luggage in the bows with the pastor's piano accordion and my sleeping bag on top. The rowers were muscular young men with bare arms, whose muscles rippled with each stroke. They sang as they rowed, their deep voices carried on the wind. For two hours they rowed in the hot midday sun. I was glad of my straw hat and I looked like a missionary from Alexander Mackay's era. Pastor Masanja reached precariously for his piano accordion. A gifted musician, he played as he sang 'Nearer my God to Thee', and we quietly bobbed in the direction of the island. It was idyllic. What a wonderful life!

Once ashore, we were given the fish meal which had been waiting for us. The two evangelists brought their cassette players for inspection, and I cleaned the heads and chased away the little cockroaches. At the church service I gave out Cassette Bible School certificates and then as usual spoke on the importance of reading the Bible. Again, I illustrated the talk with my BIBLIA conjuring trick and again there was a near riot. Again, the pastor had to calm everyone saying that Mama Kaseti was not performing magic!

Next morning we packed up and waited for a boat... and waited... and waited. There was no timetable, but even Pastor Masanja was getting worried as the hours dragged on. Finally the boat arrived and a crowd of passengers surged forward to get on board, tilting the boat precariously. I jumped off the jetty into the boat, collapsing in a heap, to be hauled upright by helpful strangers. This time the boat had an outboard motor. "Good," I thought, "now we'll be able to catch up on time." Sure enough, in half an hour we were approaching the shore.

We all stood up, impatient to be on our way. To my horror the boat didn't slow down as it neared the shore but raced onto dry land, jolted to a standstill and threw all the passengers forward. Everyone screamed. We were all lying down; my thighs had been hard hit by the edge of the seat in front of me (soon to develop two horizontal bruises). I staggered off, crawled into the Suzuki and drove as fast as I could to the church, where a huge crowd was waiting for us because it had been announced far and wide that we would be showing filmstrips that night.

Because it was Easter Saturday we first had a long, long service. Lots of youth choirs sang their own Easter songs with energetic movements and rhythms, accompanied by drums and guitars. Mothers' Union had a turn too. All the choirs managed to wear some sort of choir uniforms, including the Mothers' Union, whose babies were strapped onto their backs with matching cloths. As darkness fell, I began to hope that they would abandon the plan to see my filmstrips - but no way!

I attached the projector to the Suzuki's battery, and with the light of a hurricane lamp and the moon, we were underway. Everyone was excited to see this amazing piece of modern technology. Crowds were watching, and children couldn't see anything, so using their initiative they climbed a tree which hung overhead. I was in the middle of a commentary about the life and death of Jesus when I heard a strange creak and a groan; before I could work out what the sound was, the tree gave way above us. A moment later, dazed and scratched, I saw the projector in the dust, my assistant lying head-over-heels, and children scrambling to get upright and find their smaller sisters and brothers.

"That's it," I thought. "Now I can go to bed." I was tired out and my thighs were throbbing. But, oh no! The projector was undamaged, so they sorted out the shambles and contentedly watched the show into the night. I can't remember any more except that I slept well in the Suzuki on a lilo.

Next morning, people began to gather for the Easter Holy Communion and, if they could afford it, with an extra thank-offering and new clothes. By ten o'clock, the church was packed-out. Pastor Masanja, with his squeeze box, led the singing in his clear tenor voice, the Swahili version of...

Jesus Christ is risen today, Alleluya!

100

Our triumphant holy day, Alleluya!
Who did once upon the cross, Alleluya!
Suffer to redeem our loss. Alleluya!

A Final Glimpse in Uganda

I had begun to feel very much at home in Mwanza, but I still couldn't forget Amudat! By 1985 Amin had escaped and was in hiding in Libya. I longed to see Amudat once more, and then I had the chance to do just that.

I was on holiday and MAF flew me into Moroto, the town where I had spent my last night under guard in Uganda before being deported. My old friends met me there, BCMS missionaries Howell and Jean Davies. Howell was now the Bishop of Karamoja, and he and Jean took me to the far north of his diocese where there was an evangelistic mission in progress at Kotido. Karamoja was now bandit country, and every Land Rover had to have a huge radio aerial attached to the bonnet to summon help; it whipped back and forth on a spring over the rough roads. The bishop's crook was carefully tied inside the Land Rover just under the roof, ready for official work.

In Kotido the Mission Team took over the market space, which was heaving with tribesmen and women. Someone nearby was enthusiastically preaching over a loud hailer, and suddenly he thrust it into my hand. Totally unprepared, I sent an arrow prayer to God, and I heard myself yelling about Jesus to the noisy, jostling mob pressing all round me. I told them all about how He had helped me when I was arrested, assuming that they wouldn't have heard about me so far to the north of Amudat, but shouts filled the air: "Fancy her coming back!" and "We thought she was dead long ago!"

At last we headed for Amudat. In the ten intervening years, I had forgotten how dry and sandy the roads were and then, around a sharp bend, suddenly rocky. The breeze was a good memory too, as we drove along with the windows wide open – warm on the skin. Suddenly, we arrived at the hospital. It looked much the same as I remembered except for a huge red cross, covering a whole wall, identifying it as a hospital to marauders or escaping soldiers bent on destruction. It was a hive of activity with a Ugandan doctor and two sisters keeping things going.

I walked on over the gulley to the church, and there I saw the very same evangelist, Daudi, still faithfully teaching the people. One of the dressers from the old days, Musa, came running up carrying a hen, and he pushed it into my arms.

"For you," he said, "for coming back."

Behind one of the houses I glimpsed the old galvanised iron bath which had been in our bathroom - carried the mile from our house. It was now making a useful cattle trough.

We drove the mile to where I used to live, and I left the others sitting in the Land Rover while I slowly walked towards my old house. I saw where the leopard had broken the window, but now there was no longer any glass to break! I felt like Rip van Winkle who went to sleep and woke up twenty years later. Everything was in ruin; the iron roof had gone and bush competed with weeds to get through the doors. I stood in silence amidst weeds waist high in what had once been my bedroom. Then I made my way up the track to the girls' hostel; blackened ruins stared back at me, all overgrown by weeds and straggly bushes.

Back in the Land Rover we rattled back up the road away from Amudat. I let out a silent sigh of relief.

"That wasn't too painful."

I grinned to myself as I remembered being driven along this very road between those hefty policewomen with their Kalashnikovs.

Twenty miles along, we stopped on bishop's business near the foot of Kadam Mountain. A man with a pack donkey slowly passed by and, as I had never managed to get a photo of one, I tried snapping it. He waved his stick at me.

"You don't mind Chepocoggis taking a photo, do you?" I asked, using my Pokot name.

He looked closely at me.

"You aren't Chepocoggis; you just look like her," was his verdict.

Then I heard shouts.

"Chepocoggis, Chepocoggis!"

A big man came puffing up, and someone vaguely familiar pumped my hand up and down enthusiastically. "I thought it was you!"

Then a group of women crowded round. One of them asked, "Don't you remember me? I was one of the girls in the hostel!"

I struggled to keep the tears away. I was relieved when we rattled off again and I whispered, "Thank you, God, for giving me that final glimpse."

The Studio on the Top

I felt that I had now put Amudat finally behind me. I was glad to be back in Mwanza wriggling back into the home I shared with the Cassette Ministry. But a big change was coming...

After heavy rains, the flat-roofed hall, built onto the Diocesan HQ, turned into a sieve, and the tables and chairs had to be dragged outside to dry.

"We'll just have to get a new roof," said Ross.

My brain started to whirr.

Cheekily I suggested, "Ross, couldn't you build a Cassette Department on top of the hall before you put a new roof on?"

To my amazement he took the suggestion seriously and eventually that's what happened!

So the Cassette Ministry moved across the road from my house into the Diocesan HQ. It was so nice to have four separate rooms: the studio, with a window into the control room; a workshop where Daryl worked magic with his oscillator; and the reception where people came to change their cassettes. We even bought our own duplicator. More and more people were borrowing Swahili music and sermon cassettes. A favourite choice was teaching by Bishop Festo Kivengere.

Someone once walked into the office, holding something up and beaming, "This cassette saved my marriage!"

It was the very first sermon I ever recorded, just after I came to Mwanza during the 1976 Convention.

Mwanza was not as hot and dry as Amudat in Uganda, but it was still hot, and early afternoons in the office could be oppressive. There was just one small blessing – my siesta after lunch. But one day Bishop John announced, "Government staff never rest after lunch; it's just a hang-over from colonial times. So I've decided that we'll do the same and then everyone can go home early!" The Tanzanians were pleased because some of them travelled a long way each day, but I struggled with the new regime. I had no cause of complaint because I lived just across the road with no distance to travel. Close to my house stood the Football Stadium so I could hear the roars of excitement and groans of despair during matches.

In the ten years I was in that house, I lived in turn with four different missionaries: first Judy, a radiographer; then Avril, a lab technician; next Janet, a New Zealander who had also come to Mwanza after being Matron at Murgwanza Hospital (she was Bishop John's Secretary); and lastly Faith, a maths teacher from Australia. I picked up many of their different ways, even their twangs and lilts. I began to call drop scones 'pikelets' and to eat vegemite for breakfast, and I could say, "Good on yer, mate!" in an Ozzie accent!

I loved walking from the house to the market, my bag securely clamped to my side, following an unmade backstreet starting near the Football Stadium. All the way along, enterprising Tanzanians were busy making a living. A smell of roasting meat rose from trivets on tiny charcoal ovens. Shoe-shiners and barbers plied their trades, while men surrounded by piles of old tins were cutting them up and soldering them into tiny paraffin lamps and toy motorcars. Men and women were selling clothes which they were sewing right there on treadle sewing-machines. Wizened old men sitting behind tables sold weird looking roots, with a notice board offering cures for every imaginable ailment.

The market was a bustle of activity, covering a huge area. Everywhere there were busy people. I saw men carrying sides of meat, with clouds of flies trying to keep up. In the fish area, complete with a fishy smell, bales of dried fish were being unpacked and displayed. Market garden stalls made splashes of vivid colour: orange pawpaw, yellow lemons, green cabbages, red tomatoes and chillies. Elsewhere, undulating heaps of yellow and orange spices tickled the nose with piquant fragrances.

You would never have guessed from the hustle and bustle in the market that the Tanzanian economy was struggling; but it certainly showed in the condition of the roads. The first time I came to Mwanza in 1976, we had sped the ten miles from the airport into Mwanza Town in no time, but ten years later, we crawled. In the dry weather, vehicles had to bump carefully through deep potholes. Then the Roads Department came along and filled the holes with gravel and soil, and for a few months roads weren't too bad. But then the rainy season arrived; torrential tropical downpours sluiced out the soil and turned the potholes into pools. Drivers couldn't guess how deep the holes were, and the airport road reverted to a slow hazardous trip. The road to Nyakato to the Bible School was a similar story and precarious on my pikipiki. The Bible School pick-up was often heavy with sacks of food for the students, and it strained its shock absorbers, jolting in and out of the deep potholes. The shock absorbers broke; the tyres wore out; and the teachers, Barbara and Jenny, had an anxious wait for spares.

Of course it was different before Independence in 1960. Then Mwanza had been the home of expatriate government officials. They lived in airy well-built houses at 'Capri Point' with views over the lake and they enjoyed 'The Club' with its swimming pool. If mosquitoes became too troublesome, they phoned the Health Department and a man came around with a spray. Now no one sprayed the mosquitoes and the swimming pool was empty.

Christian 'expats' had looked after their church lovingly. They had long since left but St Nicholas Church (next door to my house) continued to have an English Service every Sunday morning, though the main service was now in Swahili and was always packed. In fact, in Mwanza there were many well-filled churches – Lutheran, Roman Catholic, 'Africa Inland Church' and Pentecostal, to mention only a few.

Secondary schools had also multiplied since Independence, and I can think of at least five large schools, most with battered buildings, needing coats of paint. The students had lively Christian Unions, and a team of us took it in turn to speak at their Saturday evening meetings which were always well attended - even Bishop John and his wife Grace were on the speakers' rota. But Bishop John was beginning to struggle with illness.

One day, the bishop called Mathayo into his office. Ten minutes later Mathayo burst into the cassette department.

"Daryl, Ruth, I have a problem!"

As usual we downed tools to listen.

"The bishop has just told me he wants to ordain me with the others next month! But I told Bishop John I'm not properly trained. I've only been to the Bible School, so I can't possibly become a pastor, but he says that's no excuse."

That evening Mathayo persuaded me to drive him to the bishop's home to tell him that he felt called to be an evangelist and not a pastor, but the bishop was adamant. So a month later Mathayo was amongst the twenty ordinands in St. Nicholas Church.

Between trips to Dar es Salaam and the UK for surgery, the bishop managed to keep on with his confirmation safaris, and I was often invited to join his entourage. I would listen to them all chatting about the old days before Independence and tut-tutting about present hardships like bad roads, lack of spare parts and food shortages.

But Bishop John would end up saying, "It is so much better to be independent in spite of all the difficulties."

Someone else would sigh and add, "True, Bishop; we never want to go back to those days. Now at least we have our self-respect."

Everybody nodded.

I learned a lot from being on safari with the bishop, but more often I was alone in the little blue Suzuki. Once, on a lonely stretch, I saw someone ahead run across the road from right to left with something waving in his outstretched arms. I slowed down curiously. A man shouted and threw whatever he was holding at the car. A huge wriggling snake crashed onto the windscreen! I put my foot down and shot off as fast as I could. The snake fell off and, trembling, I thanked God that my passenger side window had not been open.

The furthest I travelled on safari was just the 270 miles back to Murgwanza where we had a number of cassette players and CBS groups. I went to replenish our stocks of cassettes and workbooks which Rosie, a New Zealand missionary, kept (as it was too far for the evangelists to come to Mwanza). Martha - the same lady who had been the first to invite me for a meal - had been to Bible School, in between having babies, and she had amazed everyone by coming top in exams. She was now the hospital evangelist and ran CBS courses with patients in the hospital. Many other evangelists I had taught in the Bible School were also leading courses dotted around the area.

Back in Mwanza, a Tanzanian was shown to our office - not interested in cassettes but in search of an ex-pat. He just looked relieved to see me.

"There's a very sick white girl in my hotel. She's a back-packer on her own and she's bright yellow."

He used the word for curry! We went straight there in the Suzuki through narrow backstreets and lodging houses, and he led me to a slight, lethargic twenty-year-old - and yes, she was bright yellow! She looked relieved when I suggested she should come and stay with me. My nursing training came to the fore, and I gave her a cool, quiet room with clean sheets instead of the sleeping bag in her backpack. She slept for a few days and tried to drink everything I plied her with. She badly needed to get her flight home, and I managed to arrange for her to be taken by MAF to the International Airport in Kilimanjaro.

Before leaving, she showed me a huge wad of notes.

"What shall I do with all this money?" she asked.

I had never seen so much Tanzanian money in my life. She had changed it on the black market, just before falling ill. I offered to try to change it back to sterling but she wasn't interested; all she wanted was to be rid of it. She pushed it into my hands.

"You have it," she urged.

I hid the notes in a drawer and after she left, dished them out to people in need. I don't even remember her name. The strange thing is that ever since that day, I've never felt short of money - not only in Tanzania but even back in the UK. I wonder who she was?

In Mwanza I bumped into many other back-packers trekking around the country. I was also amused to see lorry loads of young people from Europe or the States on the 'Adventure of a Lifetime'. Children used to follow them wistfully hoping to be given something – a pair of sunglasses, or money, some trainers? I felt very privileged that

I had been there much longer than their few fleeting days. Yet I knew that after fifteen years I could not be here forever. We had started the Cassette Ministry ten years ago. By 1990 we had about 1000 Cassette Bible School students and one hundred cassette players scattered in village churches. I lost count of the number of cassettes scattered throughout the diocese.

Farewell Tanzania

I shouldn't have been totally surprised when, in October 1989, Bishop John called me to his office, looking serious.

"Ruth, people are asking me why I'm employing a South African!"

I assured him that I was British and had a British passport; but he already knew that my family lived in South Africa, and I could see that he was still uneasy. Tanzania actively supported the African National Congress, which was fighting for freedom from 'apartheid' in South Africa; the Tanzanian Government even financed ANC training camps in its own territory.

In the November, we had another visit from John Ball, our General Secretary. He was glad to discover that this time he wouldn't need to share a bedroom with the improvised studio that had attacked him last time! I showed him around our lovely, spacious cassette department, upstairs on top of the hall.

Next day, he and the bishop had a long session, closeted in his office. Then John Ball came with the news.

"The bishop thinks you should leave Tanzania because feeling against the White regime in South Africa is increasing. It looks really bad for him and may be hazardous for you. We don't want you arrested again!"

I caught my breath, my heart thudded and I felt dizzy... I told myself, "Here we go again!"

John suggested that I announce I was leaving Tanzania because my mother was disabled by arthritis. Of course, all my friends knew the real reason. I felt grateful that this time it would be less traumatic than when I had to leave Uganda; at least I would have time to plan ahead with Mathayo and Daryl and to say all my goodbyes.

Soon after John Ball left, the phone rang. I picked it up to hear John's voice from London.

"Ruth, can you meet a couple at Mwanza Airport tomorrow? It's a vicar and his wife from a BCMS church in Hartlepool – they're partnered with Dr Emerton at Murgwanza Hospital."

John's voice wasn't clear, but I could make out that this vicar and his wife were called Maurice and Joyce Jennett. I turned the name over and over in my mind to memorise it.

Next day at Mwanza Airport, I watched the line of travellers popping through the door into the small arrivals area, and I saw only one white couple. So I marched towards them with a welcoming smile and said, "You must be the Ferrets!" Peals of laughter broke the ice. They stayed with me for a week, and then I drove them to Murgwanza, combining the trip with a cassette safari.

We got on well, but I didn't say a word about my leaving. I took them to the airport, and as they boarded the plane, they said what visitors always said: "Do come and see us in Hartlepool!" I answered as I always answered - with a beam and a nod. With my future a huge blank, I didn't think it very likely. God knew better!

Ironically, this watershed in my life coincided with a watershed in world history: Nelson Mandela was released from prison! Even in Mwanza there was rejoicing. Every day, secondary school students jogged along in the early morning sun, doing mchakamchaka and chanting in English, "Mandela has been freed! Nelson Mandela, we welcome you!" I remembered the Murgwanza Hospital nurses doing their mchakamchaka – singing national songs and chants as they jogged around the hills.

As the day drew nearer for me to leave, I made one last safari to Murgwanza, where I was inundated with presents. Back in Mwanza, my life became a series of parties. At one knees-up, the treat was half an apple each which CMS teachers had just brought back from leave, and it was immortalised in a photo. Then there was a pudding party, a surprise party, and finally, the bishop's farewell in the hall.[1]

My one disappointment was that the 'The Jesus Film' hadn't yet arrived. This film, with dubbed Swahili words, often had a great impact on people, and Daryl and Mathayo were keen to show it on cassette safaris. A friend in the UK had bought it for us and sent it. We had waited and waited, and I began to accept that it would not arrive before I left.

It was February 1990 when I finally waved goodbye at Mwanza Airport. As I stepped on to the MAF plane, the pilot handed Daryl the 'Jesus Film' - it arrived on the very same plane which was taking me away! What was God saying to me? "Don't worry, Ruth! I can carry on my work here quite well without you." The little plane rose in the air. I watched Mwanza and Lake Victoria growing smaller and smaller, and I felt a hole in my heart; the hole was the shape of Africa.

---

[1] Not long after I left, Bishop John arrived back in Mwanza after more treatment. It was to be the last time. He was too weak to walk and Mathayo, taking in the situation swiftly, crossed the tarmac and carried him to the car. Bishop John died and was buried inside St Nicholas, now a Cathedral - a good, honest and hardworking Christian man.

Hand-wind Cassette Player produced by 'Language/ Gospel
Recordings, for work where batteries are scarce.

Ruth - Cassette safari on her 'pikipiki', to islands on Lake Victoria

Young Cassette Ministry assistant, Mathayo

Farewell gifts of a goat and a chicken!

Mathayo's ordination to ministry

The Africa-Shaped Hole

Early 1990, I was back in England after that dizzying series of farewell parties. Four Quarters in Knaresborough no longer existed. We had sold it a few years back when our different callings had led us in different directions, but I still had many close friends in Knaresborough, and I bought my very own tiny back-to-back house in Leeds with my share of the money from Four Quarters. To my surprise it turned out to be near a lively church, Anne Wright's home church. I had been planning to buy myself an old car, but to my amazement, an old friend decided to buy me a young, red Volkswagen, so I should have been counting my blessings. Instead, I was feeling sorry for myself.

My Ugandan and Tanzanian friends had always taught me that self-pity is a sin, and I remember Fellowship Meetings where they openly repented of 'the sin of self-pity'. In my case, though, I hoped it wasn't just self-pity. When missionaries come home, they often get attacked with something called 're-entry syndrome', and perhaps that is what I was troubled with. For instance, it was traumatic going to the supermarket for flour and discovering that there was an unlimited variety to choose from. Did I want white or brown or whole-wheat or strong flour? What was strong flour? There was also plain and self-raising flour and cake flour and bread flour... Then there were a variety of brands: Allinsons, Dove's etc. In Tanzania I was just glad when I could buy any flour and one sort was used for everything! Sugar was the same, and tea, and coffee, and cereals – the list went on.

As well as feeling bewildered, I was lonely. In spite of St Matthias Church being just a few streets away, I still felt different, isolated - homesick for Tanzania.

After church, people said with a warm smile, "Bye, see you next Sunday!"

I thought dismally, "That's seven days away," and walked home tearfully.

This, I was told, is a sign of 're-entry syndrome', but I could only describe it as feeling the 'wrong shape' inside. To a few people I explained that I felt a hole in my heart the shape of Africa.

From time to time news from Mwanza plopped through my letter box in Leeds. Daryl or Mathayo wrote that they were showing the Jesus Film that had arrived on the plane I left in and that many people in villages all around Mwanza were being challenged. That cheered me up!

I caught up with the Cox family in Leeds and quickly learnt the most direct route to their house on the other side of the city. Liza was as kindly and energetic as ever and Peter as kindly and placid, working in the Medical School. Of course we had a lot in common, with Amudat, their four children, and BCMS. We had to get out of the habit of calling it BCMS though. It was ironic! For twenty-five years, I had wished its name was less of a mouthful, and now, just as it seemed that I might leave, its name was being changed. It was to become "Crosslinks" because that summarised what our Mission is all about; we were not just 'the west to the rest' but part of the family of God, linking needs across the world, in all directions, through the Cross of Christ.

I made another effort to be cheerful when Kathryn, Alan's second daughter, came over from South Africa to stay with me. She found a job with the Automobile Association in Leeds. Trying to be a good Auntie Ruth, I showed her around the Lake District and the place where her father's life began - Blackpool - and for the first time ever, I went up Blackpool Tower.

As usual, I was busy with my itinerary arranged by Crosslinks and visited many churches dotted around England, from Ditton in Kent to Normanton in Yorkshire. Everywhere people asked, "What will you do next, Ruth?" I had vague ideas about Eastern Europe or Ethiopia, but missions all shied away when they heard of my links in South Africa.

I'll never forget that year's Crosslinks Annual Meeting in London. I was looking forward to meeting lots of old friends, but there was one that I wasn't expecting. As I walked into the hall, I saw Peter Lomongin, the pastor who had come to see me when I was being taken to Kampala under guard. We had stopped at the town where he ministered, and I remembered how upset he'd been then.

I ran up to him shouting, "Peter, hello! It's me, Ruth!"

There was no responding look of pleasure. His face simply crumpled up and high-pitched sobs welled up from his innermost heart. He put his arms gently around me and spoke loudly to the people milling around, looking puzzled.

"We put Ruth in jail – my country did. *We* did that – my country of Uganda!"

I stood inside the circle of his arms, speechless, and looked helplessly out at everyone. Then I tried to comfort him.

"It's alright, Peter; I'm safe now."

But he was still sobbing and repeating, "My country did that."

Peter became the Bishop of Karamoja. A good man.

Back in Leeds, I continued my usual routine of prayer and Bible reading, always hoping that I would have a heavenly vision like St Paul or that words would jump out of the pages. One morning, as I was reading the book of Jeremiah, one verse seemed to ring bells: "Seek the peace and prosperity of the city to which I have carried you." I shook my head, puzzled; it didn't mean anything to me, but I underlined it and put it to the back of my mind.

I was already planning something I'd had a yearning for, ever since I had worked with so many 'Ozzie' and 'Kiwi' missionaries in Tanzania. Now was the chance to pay them a visit! I bought a ticket via Los Angeles to Australia.

First though, there was the Crosslinks Annual Conference in Derbyshire. I arrived, rucksack on my back, and joined the crowd milling around the Foyer, excitedly greeting one another.

From the hubbub of voices, I heard someone call out, "Look, there's Ruth. Ru-uth!"

To my surprise, I saw the Jennetts (not the Ferrets!) A week later, Crosslinks phoned to say that Maurice Jennett had been in touch. Would I be interested in working at his church in Hartlepool for a year, while sorting out God's next step? I looked up Hartlepool on a map, but I wasn't even thinking about staying in the UK. Anyway, I was just about to set off for the Antipodes.

Kathryn looked after my house and I left for Australia with a weekend in Los Angeles. The trip started badly. I hadn't read the ticket instructions: "Make sure you get your visitor visa for Australia". I discovered my oversight the night before; but as I was stopping off in LA, I was assured that I could easily get a visa there on Monday morning. When I landed in LA, I discovered that Monday would be Columbus Day – and the Australian Embassy would be closed! By now it was evening; I phoned the Australian Ambassador's emergency number and talked my way into speaking to him at a party. I poured out my problem and grudgingly he promised to open up the embassy for me on Monday morning.

That left Sunday free and I decided to visit the famous 'Vineyard Church', which happened to be within walking distance of my hotel. I wandered along, gazing at the unfamiliar sight of crowds of people in restaurants having breakfasts.

Then a pick-up slowed down and a man with a pony-tail called, "Can you show me the way to the Vineyard Church?"

"That's odd," I replied, "that's what I'm looking for!"

I ended up in the pick-up and together we found the huge building.

It was too early for the service so he told me his name was Dale and invited me for an American breakfast of pancakes and maple syrup. When we got out of the pickup, I was startled by his pink and black polka dot underpants hanging down below his shorts. The Vineyard was an unforgettable experience. We waded into a sea of welcoming faces in the huge entrance; and as we struggled to the far end, more smiling faces tried to attract our interest in church plants in Tibet, down-and-outs in LA, and children living on rubbish dumps in Brazil. I wished I could stop and take it all in, but it was ten o'clock and time for the service.

The auditorium was packed, and I enjoyed being part of the vast crowd singing familiar modern songs. Then the leader announced there was to be a city-wide demonstration that day against abortion and Christians were going to form a human chain, lining the sidewalks into the city. The preacher spoke about abortion for over forty minutes - very sensitively. Some listeners had been involved in abortions and were still hurting; whenever he heard sobbing in the congregation, he stopped the sermon to pray. Then we huddled into circles of ten for Holy Communion, with wine from a plastic beaker and pieces of bread out of a plastic bag.

After the service Dale took me to lunch. Then we drove to the crowded L.A. beaches, where I tasted my first yoghurt ice cream. We sailed across the Bay on a ferry and had a good look at the Queen Mary; and then on to the hippie church, Calvary Chapel, for the evening. Dale arranged for his friend David to take me to the Australian Embassy the next morning. I waved goodbye to Dale and never saw him again.

Early next morning David duly picked me up and came in with me to the embassy. I found a crowd of people waiting anxiously in the same predicament as me; I told them not to worry because the Ambassador was on his way, and they thanked me gratefully! Eventually he stalked in and sorted us all out. David took me to the airport and I never saw him again either. Were they angels?

Nothing so stressful happened on the rest of my trip, and it turned out to be a never-to-be-forgotten experience. In Sydney, Howard and Trish Spencer from Tanzania met me off the plane. Then my friends from Murgwanza days, Arthur and Jan Adeney, introduced me to kangaroos, echidnas and koala bears and Australian wine.

I visited the Language Recordings headquarters in Sydney where hand-wind cassette players had been invented and from where we had ordered all ours; Daryl and Mathayo were still keeping them going. The inventor himself drove me to the Blue Mountains for the day. It felt like the 'outback' but it wasn't, of course; we were still in New South Wales.

I flew to Christchurch in New Zealand where I had many past Tanzania friends. Janet Baskill met me off the plane. She was also a past matron of Murgwanza Hospital but had become the bishop's secretary, and she was one of the four who had shared my house in Mwanza. She showed me Kiwis, Pukeko birds, and we drove south in her car to The Remarkables – a long range of Mountains covered in snow. On my birthday, Geoff and Carol Falloon and the Wiggins family, all ex-Mwanza, took me power-jet-boating in the Waiau Gorge. The jet-boat leapt full speed towards a gorge wall; we all screamed, and when it felt as if we were doomed to crash, it suddenly veered away, spraying a huge arc of water over us – terrifying! I think the one who enjoyed the treat most was eight-year-old Nicola Wiggins. After two weeks, fifteen 'Kiwis' waved goodbye at Christchurch airport.

Soon I was back in Leeds. My niece Kathryn picked me up at the station in the little red car. It felt cold, reminding me that winter was approaching and I must make some decision about my future. A few days later Kathryn headed home to South Africa, rucksack on her back and clutching the farewell gift from the AA - a teddy-bear in the AA uniform!

I could delay no longer. I reasoned with myself, "Nothing has popped up. There's nothing else for it; I'll have to make that trip to Hartlepool. It can't do any harm. Maurice and Joyce are good fun, anyway." I was still in the 'poor old me' doldrums; I still felt the shape of Africa inside.

The first morning in Hartlepool, Maurice drove me around the parish boundaries. I wondered, "Why's he doing this when I'm just visiting?" That evening, he took me to a meeting in the church; people in the pews beamed at me and said how much they were looking forward to me joining the team! Over supper I tried to explain to Maurice and Joyce that I wasn't at all sure God wanted me to come.

Maurice stunned me by saying, "You've been ministering to people in Uganda and Tanzania for twenty-five years; now our church wants to minister to you."

Wow! I was shattered – tearful – confused...

Driving back to Leeds, I prayed, "Lord, do You really want me to go there? It's not actually a 'city' like in that Bible verse: 'Seek the peace and prosperity of the city to which I have carried you.' Speak to me, Lord."

I listened for God's still, small voice. I listened... and I listened... but all I heard was the car engine.

Back home I picked up the phone and dialled Maurice and Joyce.

"OK I'm coming, but only for a year."

A few days later, I packed as much as I could into my little red car and headed for Hartlepool. It was a miserably cold day in February 1991.

Is this the City?

I don't know what Maurice told the Bishop of Durham, but he promised me a curate's pay for twelve months - and even a settling-in allowance! I'd never felt so rich. The last curate had just left, so I moved into the empty house and the church folk filled it with furniture. All I had to buy was a bed.

The Bishop of Durham, David Jenkins, came to All Saints for a service to licence me as a pastoral assistant with a signed 'Permission to Officiate'. Then Maurice began to teach me how to be useful. I had a list of people to visit, and I learned how to lead church services and, to my alarm, even conduct funerals. I made mistakes which the congregation took in its stride. Once I climbed up into the pulpit to preach and felt Maurice at my heels. I didn't realise he'd come to switch on the microphone. As the hymn ended, I asked him, into the microphone clipped to my collar, "Now what have I done wrong?"

It was a very forgiving and understanding congregation. Maurice had done something very unusual in an Anglican church; he had initiated a team of elders, chosen by the congregation, after much prayer and teaching. These elders became my strong support.

It was an encouraging time to become a part of this church because there were many new Christians. Not long since, there had been a Billy Graham Crusade in Sunderland, a few miles north, and our church had leafleted the streets and taken coach-loads of people to the rallies. Some of them became committed Christians and keen church members. One boy from the Sixth Form College went on to university and then became a Reader in All Saints (meaning he would lead worship services and preach). Another young man told me, "I somehow knew I would walk to the front and become a real Christian at that Billy Graham meeting, so the night before, I had a real drinking binge; I guessed it would be the last time. It was! Jeff is now an ordained minister.

Every morning I walked to All Saints' Church for 7.30 am prayers. Gulls squawking overhead reminded me of my childhood and that we were near the sea; their harsh cries sounded sweet to my ears. I couldn't believe that I was the pastoral assistant at a church where I could sniff the sea air as I hurried to prayers.

Maurice told me that I could have Fridays off, so the first Friday I followed the squawking of the gulls down to the salt air and found myself at the docks, which looked sad and neglected. I clambered along a rusty old jetty which jutted out from a dirty wharf; then I felt I'd better behave my age (I was now fifty) so I explored the more inhabited parts. Many buildings were boarded up. I saw huge hoardings hiding rubble, with 'City Challenge' blazoned across them, announcing a new initiative to revive the town and attract visitors. When I read the word 'City', I should have linked it with that Bible verse which had been haunting me: "Seek the peace and prosperity of the city to which I have called you." It took a few years for it to sink in.

Hartlepool had once been a bustling, thriving town. People were proud to be 'Hartlepudlians.' My new friends told me that each morning they used to see fleets of cyclists pedalling past crowded pavements, all heading for the steelworks and docks. They described the beautiful Co-op Departmental Store with its marble floor. Now it was closed down, boarded up and covered in graffiti. The old harbour area was derelict too and fenced off with more graffiti. Promenades were crumbling, where people remembered spending happy hours in the school holidays, playing in natural paddling pools. Everyone would tell me nostalgically what Hartlepool had been like in bygone days.

Over the next eight months I learnt more about Hartlepool, past and present; I made many new friends and began to feel at home. Then one Sunday in church, Maurice announced that he and Joyce were leaving! After seventeen years in Hartlepool, they were going to Zimbabwe as Crosslinks Mission Partners. I was left in charge. As Pastoral Assistant I had to keep things ticking over until the new vicar arrived: but it was really that team of elders who looked after everything - including me. They guided me through Christmas and New Year, until Stephen Taylor arrived in time for Easter 1992.

The Bishop of Durham kept me on the pay role till Easter, but then I made my way to the Jobcentre. They found me a job nearby as Staff Nurse in Holmewood Nursing Home, and I started working three nights a week, while still immersing myself in the parish.

I was still searching in far-flung places of the world for that city whose peace and prosperity I was to seek. Twice I went to Romania, as a volunteer with Cathy, one of the Elders. We worked in a hospice for children with Aids. The children had been in crowded orphanages and left permanently in their cots. They had all caught Aids through being given small blood transfusions meant as a pep-up. Looking after them was tough, challenging work in the baking August heat, with swarms of mosquitoes. Both times I asked God to show me if this was His next plan, but there was never a resounding 'yes'.

Back in Hartlepool, I continued to work nights in the nursing home and days in the parish. I had been there more than two years now. I began to feel my heart becoming Hartlepool-shaped! Stranton Parish was sliced into two by a busy dual-carriageway. Furthest from the sea was All Saints' Church with street upon street of private housing, mainly terraced. Nearest the sea, and the other side of the busy dual-carriageway, was a council estate and one street of private housing called Burbank Street. Being privately owned it had escaped the fate of the estate which had been pulled apart and rebuilt more than once by town planners. The people had been re-housed elsewhere in the town, but some had eventually found their way back to their roots.

There used to be many churches, but now the nearest was All Saints, our church, with the busy dual carriageway, a discouraging barrier. The area now had a reputation for drugs and break-ins. I began to feel an urge, perhaps a calling, to get involved.

Cathy Parvin, who had gone to Romania with me, grew up in Burbank area before they changed it out of all recognition. She and her husband Keith were keen to help. I talked it over with Stephen, our new vicar, and he wondered about a council flat. So when the Council offered one, the elders, including Cathy, Stephen and I, went to look at it. It was a mess, but I was eager to move in. Cathy characteristically mooched around outside, kicking the rubbish in the garden, and suddenly spotted parts of her recently stolen car, including a cassette tape of her Christian music! That decided the matter for them; they unanimously decided that, no, I should not live there!

I was a little disappointed, but Ivy, an elderly lady we had begun visiting in Burbank Street, told us of a house for sale opposite her, fully furnished. To my surprise, Stephen and the Church Council decided to buy it - number 161 - and I moved in.

Wriggling In

We started off the work in the Burbank area with a 'prayer walk'. The vicar, the elders and other friends joined me in a walk around the streets with stops every now and then for prayer. We stood in a circle and prayed near the Community House and Youth Club; next outside some warden-controlled flats for the elderly; then at the local Primary School, then the local pub; and finally on the street corners, finishing up at my home at 161 Bank Street.

We decided that our next step would be to knock on all the doors of the estate armed with a questionnaire. A small team met in the vicar's study to compose the questionnaire. They were simple questions designed to start off a conversation, like "Do you believe in God?" There was one question which I thought was silly: "Would you be interested in being confirmed?" We put it in because it was suggested by a bishop who happened to be visiting the vicarage – you shouldn't argue with a bishop, I thought.

We all set off knocking on doors and whoever was unfortunate enough to open their door, was asked the questions. I was assigned Burbank Street. A few doors down from my house, a bald man opened to my knock, and when I came to "Would you be interested in being confirmed?' he nodded vigorously, "Yes, definitely!" George was to be amongst our first people to be confirmed and he became a good friend. At another door, an old lady told me, "Oh, I belong to St James," and hastily shut the door. I was puzzled and asked someone where it was. "Oh, St James! It was demolished by a bomb in the Second World War." It was now 1993.

This whole area was being targeted by the City Challenge Project and money was being poured in by well-meaning agencies. The Council estate had new double-glazed windows. The Community House and Youth Centre had face-lifts. Derelict land was tidied up. Even our private houses in Burbank Street were given more secure doors and double glazing as part of the City Challenge. The meaning of that Bible verse finally sank in: 'Seek the peace and prosperity of the city to which I have called you'. O-o-h-h... it must mean Hartlepool!

But how on earth was I going to set about seeking the peace and prosperity of Hartlepool?

I asked Stephen and he told me, "Just wriggle in, become known and accepted, and don't worry if you don't seem to be doing any 'Christian' work."

So, when I wasn't sleeping off my night duty at the Nursing Home, I started wriggling into Burbank: at the youth club, the pub, the primary school, the 'elderly flats' and the Community House.

In early days, Cathy and I wandered into the Drop-In at the Community House and announced, "We're from that church the other side of the dual-carriageway."

The people sitting around chatting didn't look impressed.

"They've forgotten we exist down here," sighed a large lady, "and anyway, we're Catholic."

A little lady added, "Everyone's neglecting us," and looked pointedly at Cathy and me.

We sat down and chatted, and the ladies told us that they made dinners there every Thursday. I decided that was a good place to wriggle in; I went along on Wednesday to cut up a huge pan of cabbage, and the next day I was there helping to wash up.

At the Bridge Youth Club, Cathy and I started a baking class, making goodies like fudge and chocolate chip cookies. The youth leader later admitted that he had never expected them to get off the ground, but our bakery classes ran for years. The building was also ideal for Holiday Clubs. The Curate and a team of gifted young people came across from Stranton Church to help us run them; it was exhausting but worthwhile.

The pub was called 'The Square Ring'. Cathy was good at wriggling in there - confident and chatty - but I felt completely and utterly out of my element. I had to force myself to stay at least half an hour by the pub clock, or I would have been out in 5 minutes! We spent our time leaning over the bar drinking orange juice and chatting to the barmaid and anyone else leaning over the counter. It felt a waste of time, but over the next few years we got to know some of the local families, and the children of the barmaid eventually started coming regularly to a children's Sunday Club.

In Ward Jackson Primary School, I wriggled in as an extra ear for listening to children reading aloud. Soon I was asked to do R.E. lessons and assemblies. Stephen Taylor pulled some strings, and I discovered I had been elected a school governor. The head teacher and I started a Neighbourhood Watch which met regularly in the school. It was a neutral place to meet where she could be easily tipped off about local crimes without anyone else knowing. When the school received a national award for community initiatives, the headteacher asked me to accompany her and two children to the Barbican in London to receive the award from Princess Anne.

On school outings I was a useful extra adult because some of the children were very disruptive. A class once visited All Saints Church and the children didn't walk down the aisle; they just vaulted over the pews! When they got to the front, they caused havoc, and afterwards the vicar received letters of apology from the children. "Sorry I stomped on your buks," (books) one boy wrote. Next Sunday, the choir was upset when they found all their 'buks' in a muddle.

At the same time we began a Toddler Group in the school. Cathy and I joined with Anne, a mother of five and member of All Saints Church; she had lots of good ideas and experience, so it was a great success and lasted all the years I was in Hartlepool. We organised regular outings in the summer, and at Christmas many of the mothers trundled their buggies over the dual-carriageway to the Toddlers' Service.

That Community House became a venue for some of our children's activities. One Halloween for instance, we put on a 'Light Party' as a

Christian alternative to frightening little old ladies. Keith, Mel, George and Neil monitored the door and kept us all safe.

The party food was 'light biscuits' baked by the ladies of All Saints' Church - star-shaped biscuits, coated in yellow icing with silver balls. When the children had finished munching, we all sat cross-legged on the floor and I began the talk I had so carefully prepared. I spoke about Jesus as the Light of the World (represented by a single large candle) surrounded by the disciples (represented by twelve small candles). The candles were lit and the electric lights switched off, so only the candles were glowing. My plan was to snuff out the little candles one by one, as the disciples deserted Jesus, and dramatically extinguish the huge candle, as He died on the cross. The effect was ruined when one boy leaned forward and, with a single puff, blew out the lot. We were left in the dark and the girls screamed.

Some of those little horrors had Nanas living in the 'elderly flats' and we wriggled in there too. We befriended the warden, who made the lounge available for a monthly Sunday service - to the delight of Gertie, Lucy and Pat. After eighteen months we felt God nudging us to start meeting every week and the vicar managed to get us the Community House every Sunday morning without charge.

A team of young people on a 'gap year' helped us leaflet all the houses with invitations to the 10.30 service. The day came, and Cathy and I and others waited anxiously. At 10.29 not a soul had arrived. Our spirits sank. Then Johnnie popped in. He was a diminutive rascal, famous for being able to scale backyard walls, and when he saw no one had arrived, he ran off to round everyone up. Suddenly the double swing doors crashed open. It was a wheelchair being forced through the doors with a beaming young spastic girl in it, pushed by her older sister, also beaming - Emma and Lorna. Then two old ladies tottered in holding each other up - Sally and Doris. Next, someone in a car brought Gertie and Lucy from the 'elderly flats'. The vicar arrived with a birthday cake, and we were underway - planting the seed of the Community Church. Johnnie never returned!

From then on, every Sunday morning, Cathy and I arrived at the Community House an hour early to put out the chairs and to get the kitchen ready for after-church tea and biscuits and to pray. One day she asked if someone else could take over the refreshments and, to our surprise, George offered; from that day onwards, he made tea every Sunday. He had a soft spot for the children and would quietly bring them sweets and extra biscuits.

Every month on a Wednesday night we held what we called a 'prayer support group' in my house. George and four other men came to it, joined by members of All Saints who had a concern for the new work. Faithfully they came to pray, year after year, although they never stopped worrying if their cars were safe.

You could never honestly say that the church plant was a roaring success. You couldn't write a whole book about it! Crowds never queued at the door! But we never missed a Sunday, and George blossomed spiritually. He never let me forget the number of confirmation classes he had attended in our attempt to bring others in. He was confirmed with Emma, Lorna and others. Once a month we had Holy Communion during our church service, which had been brought from the main church, according to Church of England guidelines. Once there wasn't enough wine, so I topped it up from the tap; the curate was shocked!

While the older people were having their quieter, more thoughtful prayer and teaching, the younger children went into the next room for Sunday Club, led by Pat and one of the teenagers from All Saints. The children lapped up attention. There was Gemma, Louise, Marie and Leanne; then Scott and Daniel, the children of my friendly neighbour, Rose. The little girls of the barmaid and the lad whose granddad played snooker at the pub all came from time to time, and so did Daryl, Dean and their two little sisters. Some of the children lived in my street; just when they got to know me, they usually moved on - and sometimes came back again.

The vicar started giving me the names of people who wanted their baby christened. Cathy and I tried to have two sessions with them, to help them understand the meaning of it all and what they were promising to do. We had some interesting experiences such as a granddad, the worse for drink, who made it impossible to finish the preparation session. One mother always forgot her glasses, so that she couldn't read the service sheet we were going through; then it dawned on us - she couldn't read at all. Once I innocently asked a mother if the baby's daddy would be attending the service as I hadn't seen him yet. She hissed through clenched teeth, "If he comes, I'll break his legs!" He didn't.

Over the next few years, some of the elderly regulars died including Lucy and Gertie, Doris and Sally, and then Ivy. They had all been such regular members and an encouragement. They were missed. I took all their funerals. In fact, I took many funerals from the area because Stephen pointed out that this was another good way to 'wriggle' into the community. He was right; a number of widows and widowers started coming to our Sunday services and found comfort in our fellowship.

I was busy with all this when my parents, now in their eighties, decided it was time to come back to England after 48 years in South Africa, and they lived near to me in Hartlepool. Mother was so handicapped with arthritis that Dad was her carer.

I was still working at the Nursing Home, three nights a week, but the work in Burbank was taking more and more of my time. We decided I ought to cut it down to two nights, and Stranton Church would make up the difference. A year later, we reduced it to one night a week, and then, after two more years, I was so busy that I had to give up nursing altogether. The Church Urban Fund stepped in to help.

I was totally immersed in my work, yet I never forgot my ten years in Uganda, so it was wonderful to welcome one of those little Amudat Explorers who came to stay with me in Hartlepool. Stephen Kewasis was now the Bishop of Eldoret in Kenya! Nor could I totally forget my fifteen years in Tanzania. I had kept in touch by letter with Mathayo Kasagara, my Cassette Ministry colleague, over the years. He had gone on to study Theology and became a teacher at a Bible College in Western Tanzania.

One Sunday morning in 1997, just as I was about to go out of my door to get the room ready for our service, the phone rang.

Stephen Taylor asked, "Ruth, would you like to go back to Tanzania for three months?"

He had links with a bishop who urgently needed an English Teacher for St John's, their secondary school at Kilimatinde. My heart leapt and it didn't take me long to decide! A few weeks later I left Cathy and Keith to run things and set off. As I drove away from Burbank Street, my neighbour Rose and her two little boys, Scott and Dan, waved from their doorway.

This was the year of the El Nino floods, the heaviest rain for fifteen years. Rivers were swollen, roads washed away and villages cut off. The mud-walled houses had melted like chocolate and left many homeless. I had to pick up an MAF plane in Dodoma as all the roads were impassable, and I found students still arriving weeks late. Once more, I immersed myself in Swahili and tried to teach English!

The El Nino floods made it impossible to visit Mathayo, and at the end of the three months, I left regretting that I hadn't seen a single one of my old friends. In Dar-es-Salaam airport, I had passed through Customs and Immigration and was waiting for my flight to be called. Someone bumped in to me. I looked up apologetically; it was Agnes, who had been a young staff nurse at Murgwanza! She had talked her way past all the officials to see me off. She insisted on buying a Pepsi; she said a fervent blessing over it with passengers milling all around us and gave it to me. Two of her children, the other side of a glass partition, beamed and waved.

Back in Hartlepool, Cathy gave me the shocking news about my neighbour Rose: she had died one night of a drug overdose, and her little boys had discovered her in the morning. Cathy and Anne, from Toddler Group, had been caught up in the aftermath and were more than relieved to see me back. Another family had been moved into the same house.

By now all the houses in Burbank had had their makeovers. But it hadn't changed the people! There was still the same drug addiction and families moving in and out as fast as you could blink. It takes a lot more than double glazing to change people on the inside.

More generally, though, I began to notice the difference that City Challenge was making to the town – smarter, no more rusting iron and jetties for me to clamber over! The docks had been converted into a tourist attraction, with an 1817 frigate, the HMS Trincamalee, moored

129

opposite a line of old-time seafaring shops. Coaches started bringing tourists to the Quay to troupe around the Museum and experience simulated sea-battles: booming cannons and groaning, wounded sailors.

Ghostbusters!

I was well established and busy in the area when our vicar phoned.

"Ruth, when are you free? I've been asked to get rid of a poltergeist in your area."

We went to a house in the dockside which used to be the Customs House and been made into flats, and a young lady answered the door and described the goings-on. She was scared and her husband was at work. So Stephen read a psalm; we prayed in all the rooms of the flat, and then we told her about our church in the Community Centre. As we left she said she felt much better. Later Stephen phoned to ask how she was getting on; she said his prayers had done the trick and there were no more eerie goings-on of the poltergeist - but she never came to church.

There were always lots of comings and goings in Burbank Street, and I could never keep up with who lived there. One day a lady asked me to help her sister-in-law, who had just moved next door to her.

"She's seeing horrible spirits and she's terrified!"

I phoned Stephen and asked his help.

"You don't need me, Ruth. You can pray and read the Bible; that's all you need."

So encouraged, I asked Cathy to come with me and we paid her a visit.

It was a mixed up family which I never quite sorted out. We sat in the living room with Laura, her two lively little girls, a baby, and Laura's mother and brother. Laura described the spirit - so gruesome that she started to tremble. I read some verses from the Bible and then decided to teach them a song.

Be bold, be strong!
For the Lord our God is with us.

I did actions with the song and they all joined in. We prayed the Lord's Prayer together and they stumbled through it.

Then Cathy suddenly asked, "Do you use Tarot cards?"

All eyes turned to Bill, Laura's brother. He looked embarrassed and admitted it, and Cathy stood up decisively.

"Right, where are they? We'll have to burn them."

They were tossed into a metal bucket, and we all trouped into the backyard and watched them going up in smoke.

We visited that family every evening for three weeks to read the Bible, pray and sing, "Be Bold!" and the little girls sang so sweetly. Cathy and I became a familiar sight walking down the street at about 9 pm every night. People knew where we were going, and we sometimes heard catcalls, ghostly wails and eerie shouts of "Ghostbusters"! Laura's frightening visitations grew less and less, and she and her mother began to come to my house for some Christian teaching. Then suddenly they disappeared! I asked the sister-in-law, and she casually said that Bill had gone to prison and the others had moved away. We never saw them again.

I always kept a supply of used candles at home, left over from Christingle and other carol services at Stranton church. One evening Kurt, one of the children from the Holiday Club, knocked on my door.

"Hi, Ruth! We've no lights in our house. Can you lend us some candles?"

So I gave him a handful of small red candles. I realised that his family paid for their electricity by putting cash in a meter and obviously they had run out of money. He kept coming back till my supply was low. Then their next-door-neighbour came and said that Kurt's family had another problem; they had ghosts!

Cathy and I gave it into the Lord's hands and knocked on the door. We stepped into a dark hallway - no lights, not even candles. I could make out figures moving in the shadows; one was a grinning cheeky face of Kurt. There were no carpets, so we noisily clattered into the downstairs rooms and prayed. I recited some Bible verses from memory, and then we all trouped upstairs, making a din on the floorboards.

It was winter and icy-cold, and the first bedroom felt damp. We prayed. Then, into the next bedrooms, and we prayed again in each. When we had finished, Cathy went back into the first bedroom and came rushing out.

"Ruth, come in here; it's not cold anymore!"

I didn't believe her but followed her in and... I couldn't believe it... it felt as warm and cosy as if there had been central heating on - no dampness anymore. We left feeling confused and amazed.

To our disappointment, the ghosts didn't go away, so I asked the vicar to come.

"No, no, Ruth. Why should it matter who prays? I don't have any magic words to say. It's the same God you're praying to, and he hears you just as much as he hears me!"

We began visiting them every day, but then they too disappeared, and we never saw Kurt or his family again. We never heard what happened in the end, nor could we ever find an explanation for that strange phenomenon of the cold bedroom!

By the year 2000, I'd been almost ten years in Hartlepool and I was nearly sixty. I used to wonder what I was going to do for the rest of my life. No one was hinting that I should retire and I had put down roots in Hartlepool. But I had so many friends scattered around the world, as well as my ever-increasing family of great nieces and nephews.

I daydreamed, "Wouldn't it would be lovely to go around the world and visit them all!"

I felt God reminding me, "Ruth, you can't spend your whole life visiting people."

I knew deep down, that God would look after me. Hadn't He done so when I was in that cell? In dangerous situations and in small insignificant ways, God had always been there. I remembered the verse in the Bible that Miss Barter-Snow had given me at my graduation from St Mike's: "He who calls you is faithful." God had proved His faithfulness in so many ways over so many years. So I put it to the back of my mind, knowing that it would be alright.

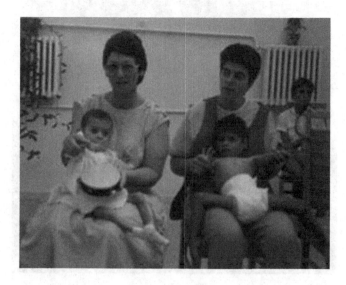

Ruth - volunteer in AIDS hospice, Eastern Europe

Princess Anne presenting certificate to school in Hartlepool

Just William!

In the year 2000, I met a bachelor clergyman who had retired to the fishing village of Seahouses, on the north-east coast of England. We exchanged phone numbers and began to call each other more and more often. We started meeting on my days off, and in January 2001, over the phone, William asked me to marry him; I said "Yes."

Cathy already knew about our friendship, and when I told her we were engaged, she insisted I tell the vicar at once. By now we had a new vicar, Mike Gilbertson, so feeling extremely embarrassed, I dialled the vicarage and Mike picked up the phone.

I said, "Er... I thought I'd better tell you, er..."

In exasperation Cathy grabbed the phone.

"Here, give it to me! I'll tell him!"

The date for the wedding was fixed for 28th April, 2001, in All Saints Church, Stranton, Hartlepool. Big brother Alan, calling it "the wedding of the century", booked his and Marian's flights from South Africa. Their two sons Andrew and James attended, already living in the UK. Julia and Brian and their five daughters had recently arrived in the country, so were all there. My father made sure that Mother was there too, even though she was still recovering from a stroke - needlework and knitting now just a memory.

William's mother had died two years previously, aged 98, and his father still lived in the village of Maiden Newton in Dorset, where they had retired thirty years previously. At 95, he was too frail to face the journey north. But William's friends made up for it. A coach-load came from Seahouses, including the Fishermen's Choir, to sing at the wedding service. William had qualified for membership by being a 'fisher of men'! Others came from his previous parishes: Byker, and Pegswood, Bothal and Longhirst, near Morpeth.

By now I had so many Hartlepool friends that it was impossible to invite all my other friends too. I was glad though to have Averil, from my schooldays; Liza Cox, from Amudat days; Knaresborough folk; and a contingent of missionaries from Tanzania days: Faith, Jean, Jenny and the Emertons and, to my delight, a real Tanzanian, Rev. Ernest Ndahani.

My father, in his element, walked his elderly daughter down the aisle, followed by my ten-year-old niece, Natasha, as bridesmaid. He sang at full throttle with the packed church. "Lord for the years, Your love has kept and guided..." It flashed through my mind, how true that was. "Lord, for the years and years and years, Your love has kept and guided me!" William, smart in a new beige suit, was waiting on the front pew with his best man, Rev. John Durnford. I was relieved to see William had his buttonhole pinned the right way up thanks to Angela Durnford.

The Stranton Curate, Linda, a good friend, read the Preamble to the Wedding Service and then Mike took over. He had already asked both my parents to step forward to 'give me away' and say, "We do." He thoughtfully came down the steps to give my mother his arm and help her struggle forward. At the right moment, my father answered with a resounding, "I do"; my mother made a heart-rending attempt which turned into a sob. That was enough to make tears run down my cheeks, but no hankie. Patti, my friend from St Mike's College days, surreptitiously passed me a tissue on her way up to read a passage from Ecclesiastes: "A threefold cord is not quickly broken." We had chosen this as the theme for the wedding day – not just William and Ruth but God too – the Three-fold Cord.

Maurice Jennett - whose fault it was that I had ever come to Hartlepool - preached the sermon. Of course he had to mention the 'Ferrets' and I had recovered enough to laugh at that. I can't remember much of the sermon although he looked meaningfully at me and reminded everyone that I had promised to obey! After the service, All Saints' bell-ringers rang out well-known hymn tunes over the town, while some of the All Saints folk rushed across the road to the Methodist church to put the finishing touches to a lavish spread which they had provided.

We spent a week at Kielder Dam - in the middle of the 'Foot and Mouth' epidemic, so most places to visit were closed. Then we began married life in William's bungalow in Seahouses. I revelled in our walks together around the fishing harbour, amidst gorgeous scenery and empty stretches of sand. I often thought, "What an amazing shore for God to wash me up on!"

Every August and December, we left Seahouses and drove south to Maiden Newton in Dorset to stay with William's father, Leslie, to give his carer, Carole, a welcome break. It was during these weeks at Cedar Cottage in Maiden Newton that I was filled in about William's background. Whenever Leslie heard me getting meals ready in the kitchen, he struggled out of his armchair, found his stick and tottered into the kitchen to keep me company.

Seahouses and the surrounding areas are tranquil and beautiful with long stretches of beaches, cliffs, dunes, sea birds and views of the Farne Islands. William's home (well, mine too) was half a mile from the sea - what a treat to live there! We loved walks along the beach, and we laughed at flocks of sanderlings running races with wavelets as fast as their little legs could carry them. How often did I repeat, "What a wonderful shore to get washed up on"?

It wasn't easy to merge the lives of two people in their sixties with very different experiences. The first year was the hardest. I became impatient when we had to confer before making a decision; it was so time-consuming! I could no longer just fly headlong doing things the way I always had done. William is much more studied in what he plans to do. He considers options and weighs up the pros and cons. Sometimes I would burst in to tears and he would look horrified.

"I was just trying to please you," he would explain.

Sometimes it would be just an ambiguous phrase which we managed to interpret in opposite ways. But we prayed together each evening, "Make me understanding in misunderstandings..." and after our first wedding anniversary that prayer was being answered; married life became more and more enjoyable.

One thing William discovered about me was that I was grumpy first thing in the morning, and I had to make a real effort to smile at him at the breakfast table. Something I discovered about William was his laugh! At a joke, or funny incident, he would laugh and laugh and laugh. Everyone could hear this loud, deep chuckle, rapidly increasing in volume. It made us all join in! I loved it.

That first year, I was content not to have a role at our church in Seahouses – married life took some getting used to! Then, after a year, William's best man, John Durnford, suggested that I tell the vicar that I was now ready to get involved - which I did.

A few days later the vicar said, "Ruth, I have a job for you! Could you cut out some paper into leaf shapes and thread cotton through one end? I want to use them for a prayer tree."

That was all he ever asked me to do.

I cried to God, "What should I be doing?"

I didn't get a distinct reply, but the thought trickled into my head, suspiciously like an answer, "Look after William."

"Bother!" I thought.

Then I got a second answer, under the one heading 'Elderlies'. Our three parents, all in their nineties, were becoming more and more needy.

My own parents were in a sheltered flat in Knaresborough with care on hand. After her stroke my mother had suddenly announced that she had changed her name from Edith to Edythe and spelled it out for us.

She told the social worker, "You see, I'm a different person now."

I guess that is how she felt. Sometimes our phone in Seahouses would ring with an S.O.S. call. I'd jump into the car and race the three hours' journey to Knaresborough.

Once I was out with friends when William phoned me about a crisis and said, "You'd better not come home; just go to your parents."

I headed south with no bag. My niece in Harrogate bought me a toothbrush.

William's father was approaching his hundredth year and getting very frail, but still able to live in Cedar Cottage thanks to his caring carer, Carole. I loved our twice-yearly visits to Dorset to look after him while Carole had a break. A bonus was that I had many friends en route, which gave us the opportunity for overnight stops and for

William to get acquainted with some of my friends. At Cedar Cottage, I continued to listen to Leslie's reminiscences, while trying to concentrate on cooking dinner.

Then, early in February 2005, my father, George, became ill. Both Julia and I witnessed his growing distress with heart failure, but even so, when he went into hospital he made sure he had his Bible and he continued his usual daily devotions. In his illness he found he could no longer read silently, and each morning and evening the other patients quietly listened to him reading his well-worn Bible and praying out loud, his voice resounding round the ward.

One morning, two nurses stood at the foot of his bed.

"George, please will you pray for us? We've such a difficult day ahead."

He asked their names and prayed for them both by name, with the volume turned up. They thanked him and went on duty. A minister/friend, Roger Faye, visited him on his last afternoon, encouraged him and prayed with him; then he died that night.

My father had requested that William take his funeral, and as he was preparing, Carole phoned from Dorset to say that his father had fallen down and had spent the night lying on the carpet. He was now in Dorchester Hospital. "Please come!" So immediately after my father's funeral, we said goodbye to my brothers, Alan, Philip and Mark, who had all come from South Africa, and we raced south to Dorset.

A few weeks later on the 6th of April, Leslie celebrated his 100th birthday! In his hospital bed he received his card from Queen Elizabeth II, a huge box of goodies from London Transport, and a Centenary cake which Carole made for the ward celebration. A reporter showed up from the local papers and the photographer took a picture of him with his new tartan quilt over his knees, holding up his card and clutching a bottle of London Transport Champagne!

Soon afterwards we were allowed to move him to an Abbeyfield Extra-Care Home near Seahouses. We were worrying about his five hundred mile journey on a hot June day, but he was pampered by wonderfully kind ambulance men, and his first words on arrival were, "I want an iced lager!" He had no idea that he had travelled so far! After six months of cosseting in the Home, he passed away as quietly as he had lived. William took his own Dad's funeral.

Meanwhile, my mother struggled on alone in Knaresborough, three hours' journey from us, with gaping holes in her care. I was often with her for a week at a time.

William suddenly said, "Ruth, we ought to move near your mother!"

I couldn't believe that he was willing to leave his beloved Seahouses, but we did move, and Mother thought William was wonderful. Six busy, difficult months followed, trying to make her life easier, until she needed major surgery in July, 2007.

A busy hospital ward is not the place for a frail lady of 92 to recuperate, so after a few weeks, Julia worked miracles to get Mother into a tranquil Nursing Home. From her bed she looked through huge windows to a lawn and flowerbeds, and she kept saying, "Isn't it green!" Three days passed, and then, after chatting with Julia and me, she fell asleep and never woke up. As Christians we know that she entered into something unimaginably better: "No eye has seen, no ear has heard, no mind has conceived what God has prepared for those who love Him!" It was a comfort for us that all three brothers came from South Africa for her funeral as they had done for my father.

With no more responsibilities we were free to go back to Seahouses - but we didn't! God had other plans. Soon after we had moved to Knaresborough, we had gone to a Quiet Day led by Peter, and a few days later he phoned. William took the call, and when he put down the phone, he said, "You'll never guess - Peter has asked me to be his Spiritual Director!"

That was just the beginning, and soon William was called upon to be Spiritual Director to a clutch of clergy in Yorkshire. My mind went back to the question I had asked five years ago ("William, what would you be doing now if you had stayed in the monastery?") and his reply ("I'd probably be a Spiritual Director.")

So we knew that God did not want us to go back to Seahouses. Also, most of my sister Julia's five grown up children lived in Yorkshire, and that confirmed that this was God's plan.

We asked, "But Lord, where exactly?"

Tranquillity of Seahouses Harbour

Ruth on zip wire ...... still misbehaving!

Pleasant Places

"The boundary lines have fallen for me in pleasant places." (Psalm 16 verse 6)

"Listen! The bells of Ripon Cathedral are ringing!" Yes, that's where we've ended up - in Ripon. That was God's answer. We look straight out onto Ripon Cathedral.

"Open the windows, Ruth," William calls, "so we can hear the bells."

We arrived in the week before Easter, and soon the cherry trees welcomed us with a burst of glorious pink blossom. Sometimes we hear the hum of the cathedral lawnmower tidying up the grounds, and we both say, "Isn't it wonderful to have a free gardener for our front garden!" And we laugh at our own little joke. It never wears thin.

The Cathedral Primary School is also nearby. The children often pass our window when they walk to the cathedral - a straggly, chatting crocodile. When I'm really old, in my nineties, I'm going to totter to a bench outside our door, sit in the sunshine, gaze at the cathedral and wave to the children as they pass by! So be it... AMEN.

Postscript

June 1st, 2010, at home in Ripon, the phone rang. I picked it up. It was Mathayo Kasagara, that very same colleague who had joined me in 1980 to work in the Cassette Ministry in Tanzania. He had been a young evangelist of nineteen then, with no secondary education - only some three-month Bible courses at the Bible School up his sleeve. He had been a quick learner. I remember that we sent him on a year's electronics course in Nairobi. Everyone else had finished secondary school, but even so, he passed with flying colours! By the time I left in 1990, the bishop had ordained him.

Over the following years, we never met, but he had done well as a student at Nassa Bible College, and then he became Acting Principal of a Bible College. He did a Theology degree in Kenya, and when he phoned me, he was the Administrator of a huge diocese in the west of Tanzania.

"Ruth, I've been elected Bishop," was his news over the phone.

When I recovered from the shock, I jokingly warned him not to get a swollen head. He assured me that with God's help he wouldn't!

"Please will you come to my Consecration Service on the 13th June," he begged.

"Oh, I'm sorry, I couldn't manage it," I replied. "My legs are no good these days; I'm wobbly. I use a stick now, you know!"

He sounded disappointed but didn't press me. Secretly, I longed to go, but I had vivid memories of the ground-level toilet facilities. Twenty years ago it had not been a problem; now, at seventy, and after a hip replacement, my joints were complaining loudly.

As 13th June drew nearer, I tried to work out a way around the problem and then gave up. I sent Mathayo some purple shirts, praying as I handed them in at the post office that they would arrive in time. Then Tim Davies, whose dad, Bishop Howell of Karamoja, had recently died, sent me his dear dad's robes – six of them on coat-hangers, zipped into protective nylon covers.

I exclaimed, "What a shame; Mathayo will only get them after his consecration."

William said, "At least email him to tell him the robes will come sometime."

Out of the blue, my friend Faith emailed from Australia to say she was taking some holiday and was going to Mathayo's consecration – could we meet in Dar es Salaam? (Faith, a maths teacher, had been my fourth housemate in Mwanza, but now she was a CMS Australia personnel staff worker.) Once again a war waged with my commonsense. I told Faith why I hesitated and she introduced me to a folding portable loo-seat!

I wailed, "If only I'd known about it sooner. It's too late to order it now; it wouldn't arrive in time."

June 5th, the day of our monthly Crosslinks Prayer Group.

I told them about Mathayo's Consecration and how I wished I could have gone. The reaction was a barrage of protests from Joyce and Maurice Jennett – yes, the very same ones from Hartlepool days – also retired to Ripon.

"Go to your laptop immediately and order the folding loo!"

"But we are here to pray," I protested.

"We'll do the praying; you just buy that loo."

I looked at William who smiled sweetly, and I did as I was told. I ordered the loo and e-mailed Faith: "Meet me in Dar!"

June 7th

William had managed to get me an internet ticket to Dar es Salaam. I squashed all the bishop's robes into a case. William rushed to town to buy anti-malarials and mosquito spray and I had some jabs.

June 8th - late afternoon.

The portable loo-seat miraculously arrived. It just fitted on top of those bishop's robes - the suitcase couldn't have been an inch smaller!

June 9th, 3:15 am

I travelled by taxi to Leeds Airport.

June 10th (thirty-six hours later)

I stepped off the plane in Dar es Salaam and the hot, humid air rushed to embrace me. I headed towards Customs, wondering how I would explain the suitcase containing only bishop's robes and an odd loo-seat. They smiled indulgently at this old lady with her stick and waved me through. I was hugged by my old friend Agnes who had been a Staff Nurse at Murgwanza Hospital when I was Matron in the late 1970's. I had seen her only twice since she married. She looked as young as ever, even after having four children.

Faith arrived from Australia. We joined forces and flew to Mwanza, on Lake Victoria. I saw little of my old haunts because we caught a bus first thing next morning, heading west to Tabora.

After nine hours on rutted roads, we arrived in Tabora, and next morning we set off on the last 340 kilometres. A bishop friend of Mathayo's gave us a lift. Much of the way was through uninhabited forest, and I was amazed to see men and women riding laden pushbikes in such lonely places. The only wildlife was baboons, small buck and warthog. Then three tsetse flies nipped in the door when the driver opened it a crack to check our back wheel, but the bishop squashed them, and I gave him one of my 'wet-wipes' for his fingers.

We reached Mpanda in the early evening. Mathayo was with the archbishop rehearsing the consecration, but his wife, Editha, ran waving towards me, and in tears we hugged; it was twenty years since we had last said goodbye! She couldn't welcome us the way she would have liked, as she too was newly arrived in Mpanda. We sat on wooden chairs to await events, sipping fizzy drinks, and as night fell we wrapped cloths round our arms to keep away mosquitoes. Eventually we were taken to the New Super City Hotel, where Editha reappeared with Mathayo and I was able to hand over Bishop Howell Davies' robes. It was God's timing - now he could wear his own robes for his Consecration and not have to borrow.

That night I was grateful for a comfy bed with a mosquito net and for the folding loo-seat! In the morning, we were driven to the sports arena where the Consecration Service had just begun. An elder showed us to seats on the platform near the clergy and bishops, beneath a brightly coloured canopy decorated with bunting, ribbons and balloons. The service lasted for four hours, but I enjoyed every minute of it, sitting in the shade, singing the old Swahili hymns again.

I counted five different choirs, all wearing colourful outfits. Each choir in turn slowly entered the arena, edging forward in rhythm, singing to the beat of amplified keyboard and drums. Anyone who was moved by their singing leapt up and waved cloths or a service booklet and weaved in and out amongst the singers, ululating to show their appreciation. Sometimes though, my mind went back to that very young man who had come to work with me thirty years earlier and I was choked with emotion.

At the climax of the Service, Mathayo swore allegiance to the Archbishop of Tanzania. Then all the clergy of the new Diocese of Lake Rukwa stepped up onto the dais to promise loyalty to Bishop Mathayo and handed him a signed copy of his vow. Some of the women garlanded their new bishop and his wife; then followed rejoicing, dancing and singing praise to God, all the bishops and clergy joining in, swirling round, singing and ululating enthusiastically. I too managed to get down from the platform and jumped around with Editha holding me up. As the dancing subsided, we sang out in Swahili with great feeling, the final hymn:

Onward Christian Soldiers
Marching as to war
With the Cross of Jesus
Going on before.

Mathayo being consecrated Bishop

Ruth being hugged by Bishop Mathayo

Printed in the United States
By Bookmasters